KT-116-593

'Much have I travelled in the realms of gold, and many goodly states and kingdoms seen; round many western islands have I been, which bards in fealty to Apollo hold. Oft of one wide expanse had I been told, which deep browed Homer ruled as his demesne. Yet never did I breathe its pure serene, till I heard *Bored of the Rings* speak loud and bold . . . !'

John Keats, *Manchester Nightingale*

'This book . . . tremor . . . Manichean guilt . . . existential . . . pleonastic . . . redundancy . . .'

Orlando di Biscuit, *Hobnob*

'A slightly more liberal reading of the leash-laws would keep books like this off the stands. I don't know how you'll fare, but my copy insists on long walks around suppertime, bays at the moon, and has spoiled every sofa cushion in the place.'

Wilmot Proviso, *The Rocky Mountain Literary Round-Up*

'One of the two or three books . . .'

Frank O'Prussia, *Dublin Gazette*

'Truly a tale for our times . . . as we hang suspended over the brink on a Ring of our own, threatened by dragons and other evil people, and, like Frito and Goodgulf, fighting a cruel Enemy who will stop at nothing to get his way.'   Ann Alaggi, *The Old Flag*

'Extremely interesting from almost every point of view.'
Professor Hawley Smoot, *Our Loosely Enforced Libel Laws*

A PARODY OF J.R.R. TOLKIEN'S
THE LORD OF THE RINGS

by Henry N. Beard and Douglas C. Kenney
of the Harvard Lampoon

GOLLANCZ
London

Copyright © The Harvard Lampoon, Inc., 1969
Map by William S. Donnell
Illustration on page 106 by Peter W. Johnson
All rights reserved

The right of Henry N. Beard and Douglas C. Kenney to be
identified as the authors of this work have been asserted by them in
accordance with the Copyright, Designs and Patents Act 1988.

This edition published in Great Britain in 2001 by
Gollancz
An imprint of the Orion Publishing Group
Orion House, 5 Upper St Martin's Lane, London WC2H 9EA

Sixteenth impression published in Great Britain in 2002

A CIP catalogue record for this book is available
from the British Library

ISBN 0 575 073624

Typeset at The Spartan Press Ltd,
Lymington, Hants

Printed in Great Britain by
Clays Ltd, St Ives plc

CONTENTS

Foreword   2

Prologue – Concerning Boggies   5

I   It's My Party and I'll Snub Who I Want To   16

II   Three's Company, Four's a Bore   37

III   Indigestion at the Sign of the Goode Eats   55

IV   Finders Keepers, Finders Weepers   80

V   Some Monsters   102

VI   The Riders of Roi-Tan   131

VII   Serutan Spelled Backwards is Mud   156

VIII   Schlob's Lair and Other Mountain Resorts   176

IX   Minas Troney in the Soup   190

X   Be It Ever So Horrid   226

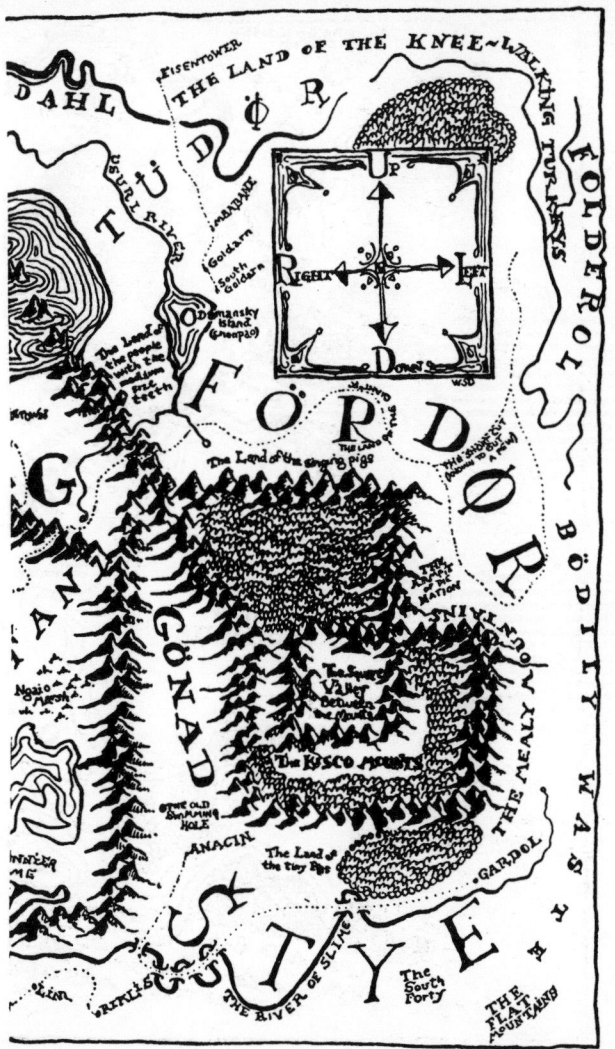

'Do you like what you doth see . . . ?' said the voluptuous elf-maiden as she provocatively parted the folds of her robe to reveal the rounded, shadowy glories within. Frito's throat was dry, though his head reeled with desire and ale.

She slipped off the flimsy garment and strode toward the fascinated boggie unashamed of her nakedness. She ran a perfect hand along his hairy toes, and he helplessly watched them curl with the fierce insistent wanting of her.

'Let me make thee more comfortable,' she whispered hoarsely, fiddling with the clasps of his jerkin, loosening his sword belt with a laugh. 'Touch me, oh *touch me*,' she crooned.

Frito's hand, as though of its own will, reached out and traced the delicate swelling of her elf-breast, while the other slowly crept around her tiny, flawless waist, crushing her to his barrel chest.

'Toes, I *love* hairy toes,' she moaned, forcing him down on the silvered carpet. Her tiny, pink toes caressed the luxuriant fur of his instep while Frito's nose sought out the warmth of her precious elf-navel.

'But I'm so small and hairy, and . . . and you're so *beautiful*,' Frito whimpered, slipping clumsily out of his crossed garters.

The elf-maiden said nothing, but only sighed deep in her throat and held him more firmly to her faunlike body. 'There is one thing you must do for me first,' she whispered into one tufted ear.

'Anything,' sobbed Frito, growing frantic with his need. 'Anything!'

She closed her eyes and then opened them to the ceiling. 'The Ring,' she said. 'I must have your Ring.'

Frito's whole body tensed. 'Oh no,' he cried, 'not that! Anything but . . . that.'

'I must have it,' she said both tenderly and fiercely. 'I must have the *Ring*!'

Frito's eyes blurred with tears and confusion. 'I can't,' he said. 'I mustn't!'

But he knew resolve was no longer strong in him. Slowly, the elf-maiden's hand inched toward the chain in his vest pocket, closer and closer it came to the Ring Frito had guarded so faithfully . . .

FOREWORD

Though we cannot with complete candor state, as does Professor T., that 'the tale grew in the telling,' we can allow that this tale (or rather the necessity of hawking it at a bean a copy) grew in direct proportion to the ominous dwindling of our bank accounts at the Harvard Trust in Cambridge, Massachusetts. This loss of turgor in our already emaciated portfolio was not, in itself, cause for alarm (or 'alarum' as Professor T. might aptly put it), but the resultant threats and cuffed ears received at the hands of creditors *were*. Thinking long on this, we retired to the reading lounge of our club to meditate on this vicissitude.

The following autumn found us still in our leather chairs, plagued with bedsores and appreciably thinner, but still without a puppy biscuit for the lupine pest lolling around the front door. It was at this point that our palsied hands came to rest on a dog-eared nineteenth printing of kindly old Prof Tolkien's *Lord of the Rings*. Dollar signs in our guileless eyes, we quickly ascertained that it was still selling like you-know-whats. Armed to the bicuspids with thesauri and reprints of international libel laws, we locked ourselves

in the *Lampoon* squash court with enough Fritos and Dr
Pepper to choke a horse. (Eventually the production of
this turkey actually required the choking of a small
horse, but that's another story entirely.)

Spring found us with decayed teeth and several
pounds of foolscap covered with inky, illegible scrawls.
A quick rereading proved it to be a surprisingly brilliant
satire on Tolkien's linguistic and mythic structures,
filled with little takeoffs on his use of Norse tales and
wicked phoneme fricatives. A cursory assessment of
the manuscript's sales appeal, however, convinced us
that dollarwise the thing would be better employed as
tinder for the library fireplace. The next day, handi-
capped by near-fatal hangovers and the loss of all our
bodily hair (but that's another story), we sat down
at two supercharged, fuel-injected, 345-hp Smith
Coronas and knocked off the opus you're about to
read before tiffin. (And we take tiffin pretty durn early
in *these* parts, buckaroo.) The result, as you are about
to see for yourself, was a book as readable as Linear A
and of about the same literary value as an autographed
gatefold of St Simon Stylites.

'As for any inner meanings or "message," ' As
Professor T. said in *his* foreword, there is none herein
except that which you may read into it yourself. (Hint:
What did P. T. Barnum say was 'born every minute'?)
Through this book, we hope, the reader may find

deeper insights not only into the nature of literary piracy, but into his own character as well. (Hint: What is missing from this famous quotation? 'A ——— and his ——— soon are ———.' You have three minutes. Ready, set, go!)

Bored of the Rings has been issued in this form as a parody. This is very important. It is an attempt to satirize the other books, not simply to be mistaken for them. Thus, we must strongly remind you that *this is not the real thing*! So if you're about to purchase this copy thinking it's about the *Lord* of the Rings, then you'd better put it right back onto that big pile of remainders where you found it. Oh, but you've already read this far, so that must mean that — that you've already *bought* . . . oh dear . . . oh my . . . (Tote up another one on the register, Jocko. '*Ching!*')

Lastly, we hope that those of you who *have* read Prof Tolkien's remarkable trilogy already will not be offended by our little spoof of it. All fooling aside, we consider ourselves honored to be able to make fun of such an impressive, truly masterful work of genius and imagination. After all, that is the most important service a book can render, the rendering of enjoyment, in this case, enjoyment through laughter. And don't trouble yourself too much if you don't laugh at what you are about to read, for if you perk up your pink little ears, you may hear the silvery tinkling of merriment in the air, far, far away . . .

It's us, buster. *Ching!*

PROLOGUE –
CONCERNING BOGGIES

This book is predominantly concerned with making money, and from its pages a reader may learn much about the character and the literary integrity of the authors. Of boggies, however, he will discover next to nothing, since anyone in the possession of a mere moiety of his marbles will readily concede that such creatures could exist only in the minds of children of the sort whose childhoods are spent in wicker baskets, and who grow up to be muggers, dog thieves, and insurance salesmen. Nonetheless, judging from the sales of Prof Tolkien's interesting books, this is a rather sizable group, sporting the kind of scorchmarks on their pockets that only the spontaneous combustion of heavy wads of crumpled money can produce. For such readers we have collected here a few bits of racial slander concerning boggies, culled by placing Prof Tolkien's books on the floor in a neat pile and going over them countless times in a series of skips and short hops. For them we also include a brief description of the soon-to-be-published-if-this-incredible-dog-sells account of Dildo Bugger's earlier adventures, called by him *Travels with Goddam in Search of Lower Middle Earth*, but wisely renamed by the publisher *Valley of the Trolls*.

Boggies are an unattractive but annoying people whose numbers have decreased rather precipitously since the bottom fell out of the fairy-tale market. Slow and sullen, and yet dull, they prefer to lead simple lives of pastoral squalor. They don't like machines more complicated than a garrote, a blackjack, or a luger, and they have always been shy of the 'Big Folk' or 'Biggers,' as they call us. As a rule they now avoid us, except on rare occasions when a hundred or so will get together to dry-gulch a lone farmer or hunter. They are a little people, smaller than dwarves, who consider them puny, sly, and inscrutable and often refer to them as the 'boggie peril.' They seldom exceed three feet in height, but are fully capable of overpowering creatures half their size when they get the drop on them. As for the boggies of the Sty, with whom we are chiefly concerned, they are unusually drab, dressing in shiny gray suits with narrow lapels, alpine hats, and string ties. They wear no shoes, and they walk on a pair of hairy blunt instruments which can only be called feet because of the position they occupy at the end of their legs. Their faces have a pimply malevolence that suggests a deep-seated fondness for making obscene telephone calls, and when they smile, there is something in the way they wag their foot-long tongues that makes Komodo dragons gulp with disbelief. They have long, clever fingers of the sort one normally associates with hands that spend a good deal of time around the necks of small, furry animals and in other people's pockets, and they are very skillful at producing intricate and useful things, like loaded dice and booby traps. They love to eat and drink, play mumblety-peg with dim-witted quadrupeds, and tell off-color dwarf jokes. They give dull parties and cheap presents, and they enjoy the same general regard and esteem as a dead otter.

It is plain that boggies are relatives of ours, standing somewhere along the evolutionary line that leads from rats to wolverines and eventually to Italians, but what our exact relationship is cannot be told. Their beginnings lie far back in the Good Old Days when the planet was populated with the kind of colorful creatures you have to drink a quart of Old Overcoat to see nowadays. The elves alone preserve any records of that time, and most of them are filled with elf-stuff, raunchy pictures of naked trolls and sordid accounts of 'orc' orgies. But the boggies had clearly lived in Lower Middle Earth for a long time before the days of Frito and Dildo, when, like a very old salami that suddenly makes its presence known, they came to trouble the councils of the Small and the Silly.

This was all in the Third, or Sheet-Metal, Age of Lower Middle Earth, and the lands of that age have long since dropped into the sea and their inhabitants into bell jars at the Ripley's Believe-It-or-Not Odditorium. Of their original home, the boggies of Frito's time had lost all records, partly because their level of literacy and intellectual development could have been equaled by a young blowfish and partly because their fondness for genealogical studies made them dislike the notion that their elaborately forged family trees had roots about as steady as Birnham Wood. It is nevertheless clear from their heavy accents and their fondness for dishes cooked in Brylcreem that somewhere in their past they went west in steerage. Their legends and old songs, which deal mainly with oversexed elves and dragons in heat, make passing mention of the area around the Anacin River, between Plywood and the Papier-Maché Mountains. There are other records in the great libraries of Twodor which lend credence to such a notion, old articles in the *Police Gazette* and the like. Why they decided to undertake the perilous crossing into Oleodor is uncertain, though again their songs tell of a shadow that fell upon the land so that the potatoes grew no more.

Before the crossing of the Papier-Maché Mountains, the boggies had become divided into three distinct breeds: Clubfoots, Stools, and Naugahydes. The Clubfoots, by far the most numerous, were swarthy, shifty-eyed, and short; their hands and feet were as deft as crowbars. They preferred to live in the hillsides where they could mug rabbits and small goats, and they supported themselves by hiring out as torpedoes for the local dwarf population. The Stools were larger and oilier than the Clubfoots, and they lived in the fetid lands at the mouth and other orifices of the Anacin River, where they raised yaws and goiters for the river trade. They had long, shiny, black hair, and they loved knives. Their closest relations were with men, for whom they handled occasional rubouts. Least numerous were the Naugahydes, who were taller and wispier than the other boggies and who lived in the forests, where they maintained a thriving trade in leather goods, sandals, and handicrafts. They did periodic interior-decorating work for the elves, but spent most of their time singing lurid folk songs and accosting squirrels.

Once across the mountains, the boggies lost no time establishing themselves. They shortened their names and elbowed their way into all the country clubs, dropping their old language and customs like a live grenade. An unusual easterly migration of men and elves from Oleodor at this same time makes it possible to fix the date the boggies came on the scene with some accuracy. In the same year, the 1,623rd year of the Third Age, the Naugahyde brothers, Brasso and

Drano, led a large following of boggies across the Gallowine River disguised as a band of itinerant graverobbers and took control from the high King at Ribroast.* In return for the King's grudging acquiescence, they set up toll booths on the roads and bridges, waylaid his messengers, and sent him suggestive and threatening letters. In short, they settled down for a long stay.

Thus began the history of the Sty, and the boggies, with an eye to the statutes of limitations, started a new calendar dating from the crossing of the Gallowine. They were quite happy with their new land, and once again they dropped out of the history of men, an occurrence which was greeted with the same universal sense of regret as the sudden death of a mad dog. The Sty was marked with great red splotches on all the AAA maps, and the only people who ever passed through were either hopelessly lost or completely unhinged. Aside from these rare visitors, the boggies were left entirely to themselves until the time of Frito and Dildo. While there was still a King at Ribroast, the boggies remained nominally his subjects, and to the last battle at Ribroast with the Slumlord of Borax, they sent some snipers, though who they sided with is unclear. There the North Kingdom ended, and the boggies

* Either Arglebargle IV or someone else.

returned to their well-ordered, simple lives, eating and drinking, singing and dancing, and passing bad checks.

Nonetheless, the easy life of the Sty had left the boggies fundamentally unchanged, and they were still as hard to kill as a cockroach and as easy to deal with as a cornered rat. Though likely to attack only in cold blood, and killing only for money, they remained masters of the low blow and the gang-up. They were crack shots and very handy with all sorts of equalizers, and any small, slow, and stupid beast that turned its back on a crowd of boggies was looking for a stomping.

All boggies originally lived in holes, which is after all hardly surprising for creatures on a first-name basis with rats. In Dildo's time, their abodes were for the most part built above ground in the manner of elves and men, but these still retained many of the features of their traditional homes and were indistinguishable from the dwellings of those species whose chief function is to meet their makers, around August, deep in the walls of old houses. As a rule, they were dumpling shaped, built of mulch, silt, stray divots, and other seasonal deposits, often whitewashed by irregular pigeons. Consequently, most boggie towns looked as though some very large and untidy creature, perhaps a dragon, had quite recently suffered a series of disappointing bowel movements in the vicinity.

In the Sty as a whole there were at least a dozen of

these curious settlements, linked by a system of roads, post offices, and a government that would have been considered unusually crude for a colony of cherrystone clams. The Sty itself was divided into farthings, half-farthings, and Indian-head nickels ruled by a mayor who was elected in a flurry of ballot-box stuffing every Arbor Day. To assist him in his duties there was a rather large police force which did nothing but extract confessions, mostly from squirrels, Beyond these few tokens of regulation, the Sty betrayed no signs of government. The vast majority of the boggies' time was taken up growing food and eating it and making liquor and drinking it. The rest of it was spent throwing up.

OF THE FINDING OF THE RING

As is told in the volume previous to this hound, *Valley of the Trolls*, Dildo Bugger set out one day with a band of demented dwarves and a discredited Rosicrucian named Goodgulf to separate a dragon from his hoard of short-term municipals and convertible debentures. The quest was successful, and the dragon, a prewar basilisk who smelled like a bus, was taken from behind while he was clipping coupons. And yet, though many pointless and annoying deeds were done, this adventure would concern us a good deal less than it does, if that is possible, except for a bit of petty larceny Dildo did along the way to keep his hand in. The party was ambushed in the Mealey Mountains by a roving pack of narcs, and in hurrying to the aid of the embattled dwarves, Dildo somehow lost his sense of direction and ended up in a cave a considerable distance away. Finding himself at the mouth of a tunnel which led rather perceptibly down, Dildo suffered a temporary recurrence of an old inner-ear problem and went rushing along it to the rescue, as he thought, of his friends. After running for some time and finding nothing but more tunnel, he was beginning to feel he had taken a wrong turn somewhere when the passage abruptly ended in a large cavern.

When Dildo's eyes became adjusted to the pale light, he found that the grotto was almost filled by a wide, kidney-shaped lake where a nasty-looking clown named Goddam paddled noisily about on an old rubber sea horse. He ate raw fish and occasional side orders to travel from the outside world in the form of lost travelers like Dildo, and he greeted Dildo's unexpected entrance into his underground sauna in much the same way as he would the sudden arrival of a Chicken Delight truck. But like anyone with boggie ancestry, Goddam preferred the subtle approach in assaulting creatures over five inches high and weighing more than ten pounds, and consequently he challenged Dildo to a riddle game to gain time. Dildo, who had a sudden attack of amnesia regarding the fact that the dwarves were being made into chutney outside the cave, accepted.

They asked each other countless riddles, such as who played the Cisco Kid and what was Krypton. In the end Dildo won the game. Stumped at last for a riddle to ask, he cried out, as his hand fell on his snub-nosed .38, 'What have I got in my pocket?' This Goddam failed to answer, and growing impatient, he paddled up to Dildo, whining, 'Let me see, let me see.' Dildo obliged by pulling out the pistol and emptying it in Goddam's direction. The dark spoiled his aim, and he managed only to deflate the rubber float, leaving Goddam to flounder. Goddam, who couldn't swim, reached out his hand to Dildo and begged him to pull him out, and as he did, Dildo noticed an interesting-looking ring on his finger and pulled it off. He would have finished Goddam off then and there, but pity stayed his hand. *It's a pity I've run out of bullets*, he thought, as he went back up the tunnel, pursued by Goddam's cries of rage.

Now it is a curious fact that Dildo never told this story, explaining that he had gotten the Ring from a pig's nose or a gumball machine – he couldn't remember which. Goodgulf, who was naturally suspicious, finally managed with the aid of one of his secret potions* to drag the truth out of the boggie, but it disturbed him considerably that Dildo, who was a perpetual and compulsive liar, would not have concocted a more grandiose tale from the start. It was then, some fifty years before our story begins, that Goodgulf first guessed at the Ring's importance. He was, as usual, dead wrong.

* Probably Sodium Pentothal.

I

IT'S MY PARTY AND I'LL SNUB WHO I WANT TO

When Mr Dildo Bugger of Bug End grudgingly announced his intention of throwing a free feed for all the boggies in his part of the Sty, the reaction in Boggietown was immediate — all through the messy little slum could be heard squeals of 'Swell!' and 'Hot puppies, *grub!*' Slavering with anticipation, several recipients of the invitations devoured their little engraved scrolls, temporarily deranged by transports of gluttony. After the initial hysteria, however, the boggies returned to their daily routines and, as is their wont, lapsed back into a coma.

Nevertheless, jabbering rumors spread through the tatty lean-tos of recent shipments of whole, bewildered oxen, great barrels of foamy suds, fireworks, tons of potato greens, and gigantic hogsheads of hogs' heads. Even huge bales of freshly harvested stingwort, a popular and remarkably powerful emetic, were carted into town. News of the fête reached even unto the Gallowine, and the outlying residents of the Sty began to drift into town like peripatetic leeches, each intent on an orgy of freeloading that would make a lamprey look like a piker.

No one in the Sty had a more bottomless gullet than that drooling and senile old gossip Haf Gangree. Haf had spent his life as the town's faithful beadle, and had long since retired on the proceeds of his thriving blackmail racket.

Tonight, Fatlip, as he was called, was holding forth at the Bag Eye, a sleazy dive more than once closed down by Mayor Fastbuck for the dubious behavior of the establishment's buxom 'B-boggies,' who were said to be able to roll a troll before you could say 'Rumpelstiltskin.' The usual collection of sodden oafs were there, including Fatlip's son, Spam Gangree, who was presently celebrating his suspended sentence for the performing of an unnatural act with an underage female dragon of the opposite sex.

'The whole thing smells pretty queer to me,' said Fatlip, as he inhaled the acrid fumes of his nose-pipe. 'I'm meaning the way Mr Bugger is throwing this big bash when for years he's not so much as offered a piece o' moldy cheese to his neighbors.' The listeners nodded silently, for this was certainly the case. Even before Dildo's 'strange disappearance' he had kept his burrow at Bug End guarded by fierce wolverines, and in no one's memory had he ever contributed a farthing to the Boggietown Annual Mithril Drive for Homeless Banshees. The fact that no one else ever had either did not excuse Dildo's famed stinginess. He kept to himself, nurturing only his nephew and a mania for dirty Scrabble.

'And that boy of his, Frito,' added bleary-eyed Nat Clubfoot, 'as crazy as a woodpecker, *that* one is.' This was verified by Old Poop of Backwater, among others. For who hadn't seen young Frito walking aimlessly through the crooked streets of Boggietown, carrying little clumps of flowers and muttering about 'truth and beauty' and blurting out silly nonsense like 'Cogito ergo boggum'?

'He's an odd one, all right,' said Fatlip, 'and I wouldn't be at all surprised if there weren't something in that talk of his having dwarfish sympathies.' At this point there was an embarrassed silence, particularly from young Spam, who had never believed the unproved charges that the Buggers were 'scroll-carrying dwarves.' As Spam pointed out, real dwarves were shorter and smelled much worse than boggies.

'That's pretty stout talk,' laughed Fatlip, wagging his right foreleg, 'about a body what's only *borrowed* the name of Bugger!'

'Aye,' chimed Clotty Peristalt. 'If that Frito weren't the seed of a crossbow wedding, then I don't know lunch from din-din!' The roisterers all laughed aloud as they remembered Frito's mother, Dildo's sister, who rashly plighted her troth to someone from the wrong side of the Gallowine (someone known to be a halfling, *i.e.* part boggie, part opossum). Several of the members took this up and there followed a series of coarse* and rather simpleminded jests at the expense of the Buggers.

'What's more,' said Fatlip, 'Dildo's always acting . . . mysterious, if you know what I mean.'

'There are those that say he acts like he's got something to hide, they say,' came a strange voice from the corner shadows. The voice belonged to a man, a stranger to the boggies of the Bag Eye, a stranger they had understandably overlooked because of his rather ordinary black cape, black chain mail, black mace, black dirk, and perfectly normal red glowing fires where his eyes should have been.

'Them what say that may be right,' agreed Fatlip, winking at his cronies to tell them a punchline was coming. 'But them that say such may be *wrong*, too.' After the general hilarity resulting from the typical Gangree gaff died down, few had noticed that the stranger had disappeared, leaving only a strange, barnyard odor behind him.

'But,' insisted little Spam, 'it *will* be a good party!'

To this they all agreed, for there was nothing a boggie loved more than an opportunity to stuff himself until he was violently ill.

*

* Coarse to anyone except a boggie, of course.

The season was cool, early autumn, heralding the annual change in the boggie dessert from whole water-melons to whole pumpkins. But the younger boggies who were not yet too obese to trundle their hulkish selves through the thoroughfares of the town saw evidence of a future treat at the forthcoming celebration: fireworks!

As the day of the party drew nearer, carts drawn by sturdy plow-goats rolled through the bullrush gates of Boggietown, laden with boxes and crates, each bearing the X-rune of Goodgulf the Wizard and various elvish brand names.

The crates were unloaded and opened at Dildo's door, and the mewling boggies wagged their vestigial tails with wonder at the marvelous contents. There were clusters of tubes mounted on tripods to shoot rather outsized roman candles; fat, finned skyrockets, with odd little buttons at the front end, weighing hundreds of pounds; a revolving cylinder of tubes with a crank to turn them; and large 'cherry bombs' that looked to the children more like little green pine-apples with a ring inserted at the top. Each crate was labeled with an olive-drab elf-rune signifying that these toys had been made in the elf-shops of a fairy whose name was something very much like 'Amy Surplus.'

Dildo watched the unpacking with a broad grin and

sent the young ones scampering with a vicious swipe of a well-honed toenail. 'G'wan, beat it, scram!' he called merrily after them as they disappeared. He then laughed and turned back to his boggie-hole, to talk to his guest within.

'This'll be one fireworks display they won't forget,' cackled the ageing boggie to Goodgulf, who was puffing his cigar rather uncomfortably in a chair of tasteless elvish-modern. The floor around it was littered with four-letter Scrabble arrangements.

'I am afraid that you must alter your plans for them,' said the Wizard, unsnaggling a clot of tangled hair in his long, dirty-gray beard. 'You cannot use extermination as a method for settling your petty grudges with the townspeople.'

Dildo studied his old friend with shrewd appraisal. The old Wizard was robed in a threadbare magician's cloak long out of fashion, with a few spangles and sequins hanging precariously at the ragged hems. On his head was a tall, battered conical hat sloppily covered with glow-in-the-dark cabalistic signs, alchemical symbols, and some off-color dwarfish graffiti, and in his gnarled, nail-bitten hands was a bent length of silvered maggotwood that served doubly as a 'magic' wand and backscratcher. At this moment Goodgulf was using it in its second office as he studied the worn toes of what in these days would be taken for black basketball sneakers. Hightops.

'Looking a little down-at-the-heels, Gulfie,' chuckled Dildo. 'Slump in the old Wizard racket, eh?'

Goodgulf looked pained at the use of his old school nickname, but adjusted his robes with dignity. 'It is no fault of mine that unbelievers ridicule my powers,' he said. 'My wonders will yet again make all gape and quail!' Suddenly he made a pass with his scratcher and the room was plunged into darkness. Through the blackness Dildo saw that Goodgulf's robes had become radiant and bright. Odd letters appeared mysteriously on the front of his robe, reading in elvish, *Will Thee Kiss Me in the Dark, Baby?*

Just as suddenly the light returned to the comfortable burrow, and the inscription faded from the conjurer's breast. Dildo rolled his eyes upward in his head and shrugged.

'Really now, Gulfie,' said Dildo, 'that kind of stuff went out with high-button greaves. No wonder you've got to moonlight card-sharking at hick carny shows.'

Goodgulf was unperturbed by his friend's sarcasm. 'Do not mock powers beyond your knowledge, impudent hairfoot,' he said, as five aces materialized in his hand, 'for you see the efficacy of my enchantments!'

'All I see is that you've finally got the hang of that silly sleeve-spring,' chuckled the boggie as he poured a bowl of ale for his old companion. 'So why don't you leave off with your white-mice-and-pixie-dust routine and tell me why you've honored me with your presence? *And* appetite.'

The Wizard paused a moment before speaking to focus his eyes, which had recently developed a tendency to cross, and looked gravely at Dildo.

'It is time to talk of the Ring,' he said.

'Ring, ring? What ring?' said Dildo.

'Thee knows only too well what Ring,' said Good-gulf. 'The Ring in thy pocket, Master Bugger.'

'Oooooh, *that* Ring,' said Dildo with a show of innocence, 'I thought you meant the ring you leave in my tub after your séances with your rubber duck.'

'This is not the time for the making of jests,' said Goodgulf, 'for Evil Ones are afoot in the lands, and danger is abroad.'

'But—,' began Dildo.

'Strange things are stirring in the East . . .'

'But—'

'Doom is walking the High Road . . .'

'But—'

'There is a dog in the manger . . .'

'But—'

'. . . a fly in the ointment . . .'

Dildo clapped his paw frantically over the working mouth of the Wizard. 'You mean . . . you mean,' he whispered, *'there's a Balrog in the woodpile?'*

'MmummfIleflug!' affirmed the gagged magician.

Dildo's worst fears had come to pass. After the party, he thought, there would be much to be decided.

Although only two hundred invitations had been sent, Frito Bugger should not have been surprised to see several times that number sitting at the huge troughlike tables under the great pavilion in the Bugger meadows. His young eyes widened as he moped about observing legions of ravenous muzzles tearing and snatching at their roasts and joints, oblivious to all else. Few faces were familiar to him in the grunting, belching press that lined the gorging-tables, but fewer still were not already completely disguised in masks of dried gravy and meat sauce. It was only then that the young boggie realized the truth in Dildo's favorite adage, 'It takes a heap o' vittles to gag a boggie.'

It was, nevertheless, a splendid party, decided Frito, as he dodged a flying hamhock. Great pits had been dug simply to accommodate the mountains of scorched flesh the guests threw down their well-muscled throats, and his Uncle Dildo had devised an ingenious series of pipelines to gravity-flow the hundreds of gallons of heady ale into their limitless paunches. Moodily, Frito studied his fellow boggies as they noisily crammed their maws with potato greens and jammed stray bits of greasy flesh into their jackets and coin-purses 'for later.' Occasionally an overly zealous diner would fall unconscious to the ground, much to the amusement of his fellows, who would take the opportunity to pelt him with garbage. Garbage, that is, that they weren't stowing away 'for later.'

All around Frito was the sight and sound of gnashing boggie teeth, gasping boggie esophagi, and groaning, pulsating boggie bellies. The din of the gnawing and munching almost drowned out the national anthem of the Sty, which the hired orchestra was now more or less performing.

> We boggies are a hairy folk
> Who like to eat until we choke.
> Loving all like friend and brother,
> And hardly ever eat each other.
>
> Ever hungry, ever thirsting,
> Never stop till belly's bursting.
> Chewing chop and pork and muttons,
> A merry race of boring gluttons.
>
> Sing: Gobble, gobble, gobble, gobble,
> Gobble, gobble, gobble, gobble.

Boggies gather round the table,
Eat as much as you are able.
Gorge yourselves from moon till noon
(Don't forget your plate and spoon).

Anything edible, we've got dibs on,
And hope we all die with our bibs on.
Ever gay, we'll never grow up,
Come! And sing and play and throw up!

Sing: *Gobble, gobble, gobble, gobble,*
Gobble, gobble, gobble, gobble!

Frito wandered past the rows of tables, hoping to find the squat, familiar figure of Spam. 'Gobble, gobble, gobble . . .' he murmured to himself, but the words seemed strange. Why did he feel so alone amidst the merrymakers, why had he always thought himself an intruder in his own village? Frito stared at the phalanxes of grinding molars and foot-long forked tongues that lolled from a hundred mouths, pink and wet in the afternoon sun.

At that moment there was a commotion at the head table, where Frito should have been sitting as a guest of honor. Uncle Dildo was standing on his bench and making motions for quiet, wishing to make his after-dinner speech. After a flurry of jeers and the knocking together of a few heads, every fuzzy, pointed ear and glass eye strained to catch what Dildo had to say.

My fellow boggies, he said, *my fellow Poops and Peristalts, Barrelgutts and Hangbellies, Needlepoints, Liverflaps, and Nosethingers*. (Nose*fingers*! corrected an irate drunk who, true to his family name, had it jammed into his nostril to the fourth joint.)

I hope you have all stuffed yourselves until you are about to be sick. This customary greeting was met with traditional volleys of farting and belching, signifying the guests' approval of the fare.

I have lived in Boggietown, as you all know, most of my life, and I have developed opinions of you all, and before I leave you all for the last time, I want to let you all know what you have all meant to me. The crowd yelled approval, thinking that now was the time for Dildo to distribute the expected gifts among them. But what followed surprised even Frito, who looked at his uncle with shocked admiration. He had dropped his pants.

The riot that followed had best be left to the reader's imagination, lame though it may be. But Dildo, having prepared by prearranged signal to touch off the fireworks, diverted the rage of the townsboggies. Suddenly there came a deafening roar and a blinding light. Bellowing with fright, the vengeful boggies hit the dirt as the cataclysmic tumult thundered and flashed around them. The noise died down, and the braver members of the lynch mob looked up in the hot wind that followed at the little hill where Dildo's table had stood. It was not there any longer. Nor was Dildo.

'You should have seen their faces,' laughed Dildo to Goodgulf and Frito. Safely hidden back in his hole, the old boggie rocked with gleeful triumph. 'They ran like spooked bunnies!'

'Bunnies or boggies, I told you to be careful,' said Goodgulf. 'You may have hurt someone sorely.'

'No, no,' said Dildo, 'all the shrapnel blew the other way. And it was a good way of getting a rise out of 'em before I left this burg for good.' Dildo stood up and began making a final check of his trunks, each carefully addressed 'Riv'n'dell, Estrogen.' 'Things are getting hot all over and it was a good way to start getting them off their obese duffs.'

'Hot all over?' asked Frito.

'Aye,' said Goodgulf. 'Evil Ones are afoot in—'

'Not now,' interrupted Dildo impatiently. 'Just tell Frito what you told me.'

'What your rude uncle means,' began the Wizard, 'is that there have been many signs I have seen that bode ill for all, in the Sty and elsewhere.'

'Signs?' said Frito.

'Verily and forsooth,' replied Goodgulf darkly. 'In the past year strange and fearful wonders I have seen.

Fields sown with barley reap crabgrass and fungus, and even small gardens reject their artichoke hearts. There has been a hot day in December and a blue moon. Calendars are made with a month of Sundays and a blue-ribbon Holstein bore alive two insurance sales-men. The earth splits and the entrails of a goat were found tied in square knots. The face of the sun blackens and the skies have rained down soggy potato chips.'

'But what do all these things mean?' gasped Frito.

'Beats me,' said Goodgulf with a shrug, 'but I thought it made good copy. But there is more. My spies tell me of black musters gathering in the East, in the dead Lands of Fordor. Hordes of foul narcs and trolls have multiplied and every day red-eyed wraiths skulk even unto the borders of the Sty. Soon there will be much terror in the land from the black hand of Sorhed.'

'Sorhed!' cried Frito. 'But Sorhed is no more.'

'Don't believe everything you hear from the her-alds,' said Dildo gravely. 'It had been thought that Sorhed was forever destroyed at the Battle of Brylopad, but it appears that this was just wishful thinking. Actually he and his Nine Nozdrul slipped out of the mopping-up cleverly disguised as a troupe of gypsy acrobatic dancers. Escaping through the Ngaio Marsh, they pushed their way into the suburbs of Fordor, where the property values dropped like a paralysed falcon. From Fordor they have been renewing their strength ever since.'

'His Dark Carbuncle of Doom has swollen and soon will come to a head, covering the face of Lower Middle Earth with his ill humors. If we are to survive, the boil must be soundly lanced before Sorhed begins his own loathsome squeeze play.'

'But how can this be done?' said Frito.

'We must keep him from the one thing that can mean victory,' said Goodgulf. 'We must keep from him the Great Ring!'

'And what is this ring?' said Frito, eyeing the possible exits from the hole.

'Cease thy eyeing of possible exits and I will tell thee,' Goodgulf reprimanded the frightened boggie. 'Many ages ago, when boggies were yet wrestling with the chipmunks over hazel nuts, there were made Rings of Power in the Elven-Halls. Fashioned with a secret formula now known only to the makers of toothpastes, these fabulous Rings gave their wearers mickle powers. There were twenty in all: six for mastery of the lands, five for rule of the seas, three for dominion of the air, and two for the conquering of bad breath. With these Rings the people of past ages, both mortals and elves, lived in peace and grandeur.'

'But that only makes sixteen,' observed Frito. 'What were the other four?'

'Recalled for factory defects,' laughed Dildo. 'They tended to short-circuit in the rain and fry one's finger off.'

'Save the Great One,' intoned Goodgulf, 'for the Great Ring masters all the others, hence is now the most sought by Sorhed. Its powers and charms are shrouded in legend, and many works are said to be given to its wearer. It is said that, according to his powers, the wearer can perform impossible deeds, control all creatures to his bidding, vanquish invincible armies, converse with fish and fowl, bend steel in his bare hands, leap tall parapets in a single bound, win friends and influence people, fix parking tickets——'

'And get himself elected Queen of the May,' finished Dildo. 'Anything he pleases!'

'This Great Ring is much desired by all, then,' said Frito.

'And they desire a curse!' cried Goodgulf, waving his wand with passion. 'For as surely as the Ring gives power, just as surely it becomes the master! The wearer slowly changes, and never to the good. He grows mistrustful and jealous of his power as his heart hardens. He loves overmuch his strengths and develops stomach ulcers. He becomes logy and irritable, prone to neuritis, neuralgia, nagging backache, and frequent colds. Soon no one invites him to parties anymore.'

'A most horrible treasure, this Great Ring,' said Frito.

'And a horrible burden for he who bears it,' said Goodgulf. 'For some unlucky one must carry it from Sorhed's grasp into danger and certain doom. Someone must take the ring to the Zazu Pits of Fordor, under the evil nose of the wrathful Sorhed, yet appear so unsuited to his task that he will not be soon found out.'

Frito shivered in sympathy for such an unfortunate. 'Then the bearer should be a complete and utter dunce,' he laughed nervously.

Goodgulf glanced at Dildo, who nodded and casually flipped a small, shining object into Frito's lap. It was a ring.

'Congratulations,' said Dildo somberly. 'You've just won the booby prize.'

II

THREE'S COMPANY,
FOUR'S A BORE

'If I were thee,' said Goodgulf, 'I would start on thy journey soon.' Frito looked up absently from his rutabaga tea.

'For half a groat you *can* be me, Goodgulf. I don't remember volunteering for this Ring business.'

'This is not the time for idle banter,' said the Wizard, pulling a rabbit from his battered hat. 'Dildo left days ago and awaits you at Riv'n'dell, as will I. There the fate of the Ring will be decided by all the peoples of Lower Middle Earth.'

Frito pretended to be engrossed in his cup as Spam entered from the dining room and began tidying up the hole, packing up the last of Dildo's belongings for storage.

'Lo, Master Frito,' he rasped, pulling a greasy forelock. 'Just gettin' the rest o' the stuff together for your uncle what mysteriously disappeared wi'out a trace. Strange business that, eh?' Seeing that no explanation was forthcoming, the faithful servant shuffled off into Dildo's bedroom. Goodgulf, hastily retrieving his rabbit, who was being loudly sick on the carpet, resumed speaking.

'Are you sure he can be trusted?'

Frito smiled. 'Of course. Spam's been a true friend of mine since we were weanlings at obedience school together.'

'And he knows nothing of the Ring?'

'Nothing,' said Frito. 'I am sure of it.'

Goodgulf looked dubiously toward the closed door of the bedroom. 'You still have it, don't you?'

Frito nodded and fished out the chain of paper clips that secured it to his tattersall bowling shirt.

'Then be careful with it,' said Goodgulf, 'for it has many strange powers.'

'Like turning my pocket green?' asked the young boggie, turning the small circlet in his stubby fingers. Fearfully he stared at it, as he had so many times in the past few days. It was made of bright metal and was encrusted with strange devices and inscriptions. Around the inner surface was written something in a language unknown to Frito.

'I can't make out the words,' said Frito.

'No, you cannot,' said Goodgulf. 'They are elvish, in the tongue of Fordor. A rough translation is:

> *This Ring, no other, is made by the elves,*
> *Who'd pawn their own mother to grab it themselves.*
> *Ruler of creeper, mortal, and scallop,*
> *This is a sleeper that packs quite a wallop.*

The Power almighty rests in this Lone Ring.
The Power, alrighty, for doing your Own Thing.
If broken or busted, it cannot be remade
If found, send to Sorhed (the postage is prepaid).

'Shakestoor, it isn't,' said Frito, hurriedly putting the Ring back in his shirt pocket.

'But a dire warning nonetheless,' said Goodgulf. 'Even now Sorhed's tools are abroad sniffing for this ring, and the time grows short before they smell it here. It is the time to set off for Riv'n'dell.' The old magician stood, walked to the bedroom door, and opened it with a jerk. With a heavy crash, Spam fell forward ear first, his pockets full of Dildo's best mithril-plate tablespoons. 'And *this* will be your faithful companion.' As Goodgulf passed into the bedroom, Spam grinned sheepishly at Frito with a lop-eared stupidity Frito had learned to love, futilely trying to hide the spoons in his pockets.

Ignoring Spam, Frito called fearfully after the Wizard.

'But – but – there are still many preparations I must make! My bags—'

'Have no worry,' said Goodgulf as he held out two valises. 'I took the precaution of packing them for you.'

The night was as clear as an elfstone, sparkling with

starpoints, as Frito gathered his party in the pasture outside the town. In addition to Spam, were the twin brothers Moxie and Pepsi Dingleberry, both of whom were noisome and easily expendable. They were frisking happily in the meadow. Frito called them to attention, wondering vaguely why Goodgulf had saddled him with two tail-wagging idiots that no one in the town could trust with a burnt-out match.

'Let's go, let's go!' cried Moxie.

'Yes, *let's*,' added Pepsi, who promptly took one step, fell directly on his flat head, and managed to bloody his nose.

'Icky!' laughed Moxie.

'*Double* icky!' wailed Pepsi.

Frito rolled his eyes heavenward. It was going to be a long epic.

Gaining their wandering attention, Frito inspected his companions and their kits. As he had feared, his orders had been forgotten and everyone had brought the potato salad. Everyone except Spam, who had stuffed his knapsack with sleazy novels and Dildo's tablespoons.

At last they set off, following Goodgulf's instructions, along the yellow-brick Intershire Turnpath toward Whee, the longest leg of their journey to Riv'n'dell. The Wizard had told them to travel at night unseen along the side of the Path, to keep their ear to the ground, their eyes peeled and their noses clean, the last directive weighing rather heavily on Pepsi, under the circumstances.

For a while they walked along in silence, each lost in what passed in boggies for thought. But Frito was especially troubled as he considered the long travels ahead of him. Though his companions frisked gaily along, playfully kicking and tripping each other, his heart was heavy with dread. Remembering happier times, he hummed and then sang an ancient dwarf-song he had learned from the knee of his Uncle Dildo, a song whose maker had lived before the dawn of Lower Middle Earth. It began:

> Heigh-ho, heigh-ho,
> It's off to work we go,
> Heigh-ho, heigh-ho, heigh-ho, heigh-heigh,
> Heigh-ho, heigh-ho . . .

'Good! Good!' yipped Moxie.

'Yes, good! Especially the "heigh-ho" part,' added Pepsi.

'And what do you be callin' that?' asked Spam, who knew few songs.*

'I call it "Heigh-ho," ' said Frito.

But he was not cheered by it.

---

* Clean ones, at least.

Soon it began to rain and they all caught colds.

The sky in the east was changing from black to pearl-gray as the four boggies, weary and sneezing their heads off, stopped their march and camped for the day's rest in a clump of dogwillows many steps from the unprotected Turnpath. The fatigued travelers stretched out on the sheltered ground and made a long boggie snack from Frito's store of dwarfloaf, boggie-brewed ale, and breaded veal cutlets. Then, groaning softly under the weight of their stomachs, all dropped quickly off to sleep, each dreaming their private boggie dreams, most of them having to do with veal cutlets.

Frito awoke with a start. It was dusk now, and a sick feeling in his stomach made him scan the Path from between the branches with terror. Through the leaves he saw a dark, shadowy bulk in the distance. It moved slowly and carefully along the rise of the Path, looking like a tall, black rider on some huge and bloated beast. Outlined against the setting sun, Frito held his breath as the ominous figure's red eyes searched the land. Once, Frito thought, the fiery coals had looked right through him, but they blinked myopically and passed on. The ponderous mount, which appeared to Frito's startled eyes to be an immense, grossly overfed pig the size of a house, snuffled and snorted in the wet earth to root out some scent of them. The others awoke and froze with terror. As they watched, the evil hunter goaded his mount, emitted one great and sour fart, and passed on. He had not seen them.

The boggies waited until the distant grunting of the beast had long quieted before anyone spoke. Frito turned to his companions, who were well hidden in their foodsacks, and whispered, 'It's all right. It's gone.'

Doubtfully, Spam emerged. 'Bless me if that didn't fright me plumb out o' me codpiece,' laughed Spam weakly. 'Most queer and disturbin'!'

'Queer and disturbin'!' came a chorus of voices from the other sacks.

'And even more disturbin' if I keep on a-hearin' me echo every time I open me chops!' Spam kicked the sacks, each of which yelped, but showed no sign of disgorging its contents.

'Grouchy, he is,' said one.

'Grouchy and *mean*,' said the other.

'I wonder,' said Frito, 'what and who that terrible creature was.'

Spam cast his eyes downward and scratched his chins guiltily. 'I'm guessin' it's one o' those folk the Fatlip told me to remember to be a-warnin' ye about, Master Frito.'

Frito looked at him inquiringly.

'Weeeell,' said Spam, pulling his forelock and

licking Frito's toes in apology, 'as I recollect now, the Old Lip was a-tellin' me just before we left, *And don't be forgettin'*, he says to me, *to tell Master Frito that some smelly stranger wi' red eyes was askin' after him. Stranger?* says I. *Aye*, says he, *and when I keeps mum, the fiend up and hisses at me and twirls 'is black mustache. "Curses," the foul thing says, "foiled again!" And then he waves 'is billy at me and jumps on 'is pig and hightails it fræ th' Bag Eye a-shoutin' somethin' very much like "Hi-yo Slimey!"* Very strange, I says. I guess I was a bit slow t' tell ye, Master Frito.'

'Well,' said Frito, 'there's no time to worry now. I'm not sure, but I wouldn't be surprised if there's some connection between that stranger and this foul searcher.' Frito knitted his brows, but as usual dropped a stitch. 'In any case,' he said, 'it's no longer safe to follow the Turnpath to Whee. We'll have to take the shortcut through the Evilyn Wood.'

'The Evilyn Wood!?' chorused the grubsacks.

'But Master Frito,' said Spam, 'they say that place is . . . *haunted*!'

'That may be true,' said Frito quietly, 'but if we stay here, we're all blue-plate specials for sure.'

Frito and Spam hastily decanted the twins with hearty kicks, and the company policed the remaining fragments of cutlets from the area, spicing the left-overs with a number of sawbugs. When all was ready, they set out, the twins emitting high-pitched *cheep-cheeps* in the not altogether vain hope of passing themselves off in the dark as migrating cockroaches. Due west they tramped, doggedly locating every possible opportunity for falling flat on their muzzles, pressing on so that they might reach the safety of the wood before the next sunrise. Frito had calculated that they traveled over two leagues in as many days, not bad for a boggie but still not fast enough. They had to take the wood in stride to be at Whee by the next day.

Silently they walked, save for a slight whimpering from Pepsi. *The silly nit's bloodied his pug again*, thought Frito, *and Moxie's getting cranky*. But as the long night passed and the east brightened, the flat ground gave way to hummocks, hillocks, and buttocks of spongy, soft earth the color of calves' brains. As the company stumbled on, the underbrush changed to saplings and then to huge, irritable-looking trees, blasted and scored by wind, weather, and arthritis. Soon they were swallowed up from the dawn light, and the new night covered them like a rank locker-room towel.

Many years before it had been a happy, pleasant forest of well-pruned puswillows, spruce spruces, and natty pines, the frolicking place of drone-moles and slightly rabid chipmunks. But now the trees had grown old, clotted with sneezemoss and toemold, and the Nattily Wood had become the crotchety old Evilyn.

'We should be in Whee by morning,' said Frito as they paused for a light snack of potato salad. But the malevolent susurrus in the trees over the small company bade them not tarry there long. They quickly moved on, careful to avoid the occasional barrages of droppings that fell from unseen, yet annoyed tenants in the branches above.

After several hours of mucking about, the boggies fell exhausted to the ground. The ground was unfamiliar to Frito, and he had long since muddled his sense of direction. 'We should have been out of these woods by now,' he said worriedly. 'I think we're lost.'

Spam looked at his rapier-sharp toenails in dejection, but then brightened. 'That may be true, Master Frito,' he said. 'But don't be a-worryin' about it. Somebody else was here only a few hours ago, by the looks o' the camp. An' they was gobblin' tater salad just like us!'

Frito studied these telltale clues with care. It was true, someone had been here only a few hours before, lunching on boggie grub. 'Perhaps we can follow their trail and find the way out of here.' And tired as they were, they pushed on again.

On and on they trod, vainly calling after the folk whose evidence of passage lay after them: a scrap of breaded veal cutlet, a sleazy boggie novel, one of

Dildo's tablespoons (*What a coincidence*, Frito thought.)
But no boggies. They did come across a large rabbit
with a cheap pocket watch who was pursued by some
nut of a girl, another kid being viciously mugged by
three furious grizzlies ('We'd better not get involved,'
said Frito wisely), and a deserted and flyspecked
gingerbread bungalow with a 'To Let' sign on the
marzipan door. But no clue to a way out.

Limp with fatigue, the four finally dropped in their
tracks. It was already late afternoon in the gloomy
woods, and they could go no farther without a snooze.
As if lulled by a potion, the hairy little beggars curled
up in furry balls and, one by one, conked off under the
protective boughs of a huge, quivering tree.

Spam did not at first realize he was awake. He had
felt something soft and rubbery pull at his clothes, but
he thought it a longing dream of those reptilian
pleasures he had so recently enjoyed back in the Sty.
But now he was certain he had heard a distinct *sucking*
sound and a tearing of cloth. His eyes popped open to
see himself stark naked and bound head and paw by the
fleshy roots of the tree. Screaming his fool head off, he
woke his fellows, likewise hogtied and stripped clean
by the writhing plant, which was giving off a distinct
cooing noise. The strange tree hummed to itself, ever
tightening its hold. As the boggies watched with
revulsion, the crooning tossed salad dipped down the

orangy, liplike flowers at its tips. The bulbous pods drew nearer, making revolting *smacking* and *smooching* noises as they began to fasten themselves to their helpless bodies. Locked in a foul embrace, the boggies would soon be hickeyed to death. Summoning their last strength, they all cried for help.

'Help, help!' they cried.

But no one answered. The fat orange blossoms ranged over their helpless boggie bodies, squirming and moaning with desire. A bloated blossom fastened to Spam's boggie belly and began its relentless sucking motion; he felt his flesh drawn up to the center of the flower. Then, as Sam looked on in horror, the petals released with a resounding *pop*!, leaving a dark, malignant weal where the horrid pucker had been. Spam, powerless to save himself or his companions, watched terrified as the now-panting sepals prepared to administer their final, deadly soul kiss.

But just as the long, red stamen descended to its unspeakable task, Spam thought he heard the snatch of a lilting song not far distant, and growing louder! It was a muddled, drowsy voice that sang words that were not words to Spam's ears:

> *Toke-a-lid! Smoke-a-lid! Pop the mescalino!*
> *Stash the hash! Gonna crash! Make mine methedrino!*
> *Hop a hill! Pop a pill! For Old Tim Benzedrino!*

Though mad with fear, all strained to the rising melody sung by someone who sounded like he had terminal mumps:

Snorting, sporting! Speeding through the arbor,
Pushing till the folk you burn toss you in the harbor!
Screeching like a dying loon, zooming like the thrush!
Follow me and very soon, your mind will turn to mush!
Higher than the nowhere birds grooving in the air,
We'll open up a sandal shop where everyone will share!
Flower folk are springing up, wearing bead and boot,
And if you down me you can stick a flower up your
    snoot!
To Love and Peace and Brotherhood we all can snort a
    toast,
And if the heat is on again, we'll all split to the Coast!

Suddenly a brightly colored figure burst through the foliage, swathed in a long mantle of hair the consistency of much-chewed Turkish taffy. It was something like a man, but not much; it stood six feet tall, but could not have weighed more than thirty-five pounds, dirt included. Standing with his long arms dangling almost to the ground, the singer's body was covered with a pattern of startling hues, ranging from schizoid red to psychopathique azure. Around his pipestem neck hung a dozen strands of beaded charms and from the center, an amulet imprinted with the elf-rune *Kelvinator*. Through the oily snaggles of hair stared two huge eyeballs that bulged from their sockets, so bloodshot that they appeared more like two baseballs of very lean bacon.

'Ooooooooooh, wow!' said the creature, assaying the situation quickly. Then, half loping, half rolling to the foot of the murderous tree, he sat on his meatless haunches and peered at it with his colorless, saucerlike irises; he chanted an incantation that sounded to Frito like a hacking cough:

> *Oh uncool bush! Unloose this passle*
> *Of furry cats that you hassle!*
> *Tho' by speed my brain's destroyed,*
> *I'm not half this paranoid!*
> *So cease this bummer, down the freak-out,*
> *Let caps and joints cause brains to leak-out!*
> *These cats are groovy here among us,*
> *So leave 'em be, you uptight fungus!*

Thus speaking, the withered apparition raised his spidery hand in a two-fingered 'V' sign and uttered an eldritch spell:

> *Tim, Tim, Benzedrine!*
> *Hash! Boo! Valvoline!*
> *Clean! Clean! Clean for Gene!*
> *First, second, neutral, park,*
> Hie thee hence, *you leafy narc!*

The towering plant shivered and the coils fell from its victims like yesterday's macaroni, and they sprang free with joyful yelps. As they watched with fascination, the great green menace whimpered like a nursling and sucked its own pistils with ill temper. The boggies retrieved their garments, and Frito sighed with relief to find the Ring still firmly Bostiched to his pocket.

'Oh thank you,' they all squealed, wagging their tails, 'thank you, thank you!' But their savior said nothing. As if unaware of their presence, he stiffened like the tree and gasped, 'Gah gah gah' while his pupils opened and closed like nervous umbrellas. His knees buckled and unbuckled, then buckled again and he fell to the mossy earth in a ball of frantically thrashing hair. He foamed at the mouth and screamed, 'Oh, God get 'em off me! They're all over the place, and green! Argh! Org! *OhGodOhGodOhGodOhGodOhGodOhGod!*' He slapped at his hair and body hysterically.

Frito blinked with astonishment and grabbed his Ring, but did not put it on. Spam, stooping over the prostrate freak, smiled and offered his hand.

'Beggin' your leave,' he said, 'can you tell us where—'

'Oh no no *no*! Look at all of 'em! All over the place! *Keep 'em away from me!*'

'Keep who away?' asked Moxie politely.

'*Them!*' screamed the stricken stranger, pointing to

his own head. He then sprang to his horny feet and ran directly at the trunk of the hickey tree and, charging full tilt with his head lowered, butted it a mighty lick, and, before the startled eyes of the boggies, passed out cold. Frito filled his narrow-brimmed hat with clear water from a nearby trickle and approached him, but the stunned figure opened his marbled eyes and gave another high-pitched scream.

'No, no, not *water!*'

Frito jumped back with fright and the skinny creature wobbled to his feet and knuckles.

'But thangs loads anyhoo,' said the stranger, 'the rush always arfects me like dat.' Offering a filthy hand, the odd-speaking stranger smiled a toothless grin. 'Tim Benzedrine, ad yer serbice.'

Frito and the rest solemnly introduced themselves, all still casting a worried eye toward the kissing plant, which was sticking out its stamen at them.

'Oh wow, doan' worby about him,' wheezed Tim, 'he just sulking. Yoo cats noo aroun' here?'

Frito guardedly told him that they were on their way to Whee, but had become lost. 'Can you tell us how to find our way there?'

'Oh wow, oh sure,' laughed Tim, 'thad's easy. But led's split to my pad firz, I wan' yoo meet my chick. She name Hashberry.'

The boggies agreed, for their stores of potato salad

were gone. Gathering their packs, they curiously followed after the wildly zigzagging Benzedrine, who occasionally halted to rap with a likely looking rock or stump, giving them time to catch up. As they circled through the menacing trees aimlessly, Tim Benzedrine's throat croaked merrily:

O slender as a speeding freak! Spaced-out groovy tripper!
O mush-brained maid whose mind decays with every
    pill I slip her!
O mind-blown fair farina-head, friend of birds and
    beetles!
O skinny wraith whose fingernails are hypodermic needles!
O tangled locks and painted bod! Pupils big as eggs!
O flower-maid who never bathes or even shaves her legs!
O softened mind that wanders wherever moon above
    leads!
O how I dig thee, Hashberry, from nose to sleazy love-
    beads!

A few moments later they broke into a clearing on a low hill. There was a ramshackle hovel shaped like a rubber boot with a little chimney that emitted a thick fog of sick-looking green smoke.

'Oh wow,' squeaked Tim, 'she's home!' Led by Tim, the company approached the unprepossessing little hut. A flashing white light blinked from its only window, at the top. As they stepped over the threshold, littered with cigarette papers, broken pipes, and burnt-out brain cells, Tim called:

> *I've brought four with me to crash,*
> *So now's the time to pass the stash.*

From the smoky depths an answering voice returned:

> *Then celebrate and take a toke,*
> *To make us giggle, gag and choke!*

At first Frito saw nothing amid the iridescent wallpaper and strobe candles but what appeared to be a heap of filthy cleaning rags. But then the pile spoke again:

> *Hither come and suck a pipe,*
> *Turn thy brains to cheese and tripe!*

And then, as the boggies squinted their smarting eyes, the heap stirred and sat up revealing itself to be an incredibly emaciated, hollow-eyed female. She looked at them for a second, muttered, 'Like wow,' and fell forward in a catatonic stupor with a rattle of beads.

'Doan' let Hash bug yoo,' said Tim. 'Tuesday is her day to crash.'

Somewhat bewildered by the acrid fumes and the flashing candles, the boggies sat crosslegged on a grimy mattress and asked politely for some grub, as they had journeyed far and were about to devour the ticking.

'Eats?' chuckled Tim, rummaging through a hand-made leather pouch. 'Jes' hang loose an' I'll fimb somp'un f'yoo. Lemmesee, oh, oh wow! Dint know we had any this left!' Clumsily he scooped out the contents and set them in a bent hubcap before them. They were among the most dubious-looking mushrooms Spam had ever seen, and, rather rudely, he said so.

'These are among the most dubious-lookin' mushrooms I'm ever a-seeing,' he stated.

Nevertheless there were few things in Lower Middle Earth Spam *hadn't* idly nibbled and lived to tell about, so he dived in, stuffing himself loudly. They were of an odd color and odor, but they tasted okay, if a little on the moldy side, and after that the boggies were offered round candies with little letters cleverly printed on them. ('They melt in yoor brain, not in your hans,' giggled Tim.)

Bloated to critical mass, the contented boggies relaxed as Hashberry played a melody on something that looked like a pregnant handloom. Mellowed by the repast, Sam was particularly pleased when Tim offered him some of his 'own speshul mix' for his nose-pipe. An odd flavor, thought Spam, but nice.

'Yoo got about ha'f an hour,' said Tim. 'Wanna rap?'

'Rap?' said Spam.

'Yoo know, like . . . talk wif your mouf,' replied

Tim as he lit his own pipe, a large converted milk separator laden with valves and dials. 'Yoo here 'cause th' heat's on?'

'In a manner of speaking,' said Frito judiciously. 'We've got this here Ring of Power and – oops!' Frito caught himself, but too late; he could not unsay it now.

'Oh groovy!' said Tim. 'Lemme see.'

Reluctantly, Frito handed over the Ring.

'Pretty cheap stuff,' said Tim, tossing it back. 'Even th' junk I pawn off on th' dwarbs is bedder.'

'You sell rings?' asked Moxie.

'Sure,' said Tim. 'I gotta sandal-and-magic-charm shop for th' tourist season. Keeps me in stash for winter months, y'know whad I mean?'

'There might not be many of us left to visit the woods,' said Frito quietly, 'if Sorhed's plans are not foiled. Will you join us?'

Tim shook his hair. 'Now doan' bug me, man. I'm a conscienshul objectioner . . . doan' wan' no more war. Came here to dodge draff, see? If some cat wants to kick th' stuffing outta me, I say, "Groovy," an' I give 'em a flower an' love-beads. "Love," I say t' him. "No more war," I say. Anyway, I four-F!'

'No more guts!' growled Spam under his breath to Moxie.

'No, I *god* guts,' said Tim, pointing to his temple, 'no more braims!'

Frito smiled diplomatically, but was suddenly stricken by a severe stomachache. His eyes began to roll and he felt very light-headed. *Probably a touch of the banshee two-step*, he thought as his ears started to ring like a dwarf's cash-register. His tongue felt thick, and his tail began to vibrate. Turning to Spam, he wished to ask him if he felt it too.

'Argle-bargle morble whoosh?' said Frito.

But it did not matter, for he saw that Spam had oddly taken it into his head to change himself into a large, pink dragon wearing a three-piece suit and a straw boater.

'What did you be sayin', Master Frito?' asked the natty lizard with Spam's voice.

'Ffluger fribble golorful frooble,' said Frito dreamily, thinking it strange that Spam was wearing a boater in late autumn. Glancing at the twins, Frito noted that they had changed into matching candy-striped coffee-pots perking away like mad.

'Don't feel too well,' said one.

'Feel *sick*,' clarified the other.

Tim, now a rather handsome six-foot carrot, laughed loudly and changed into a coiled parking meter. Frito, dizzy as a great wave of oatmeal flowed through his brain, grew heedless of the puddle of drool collecting in his lap. There was a noiseless explosion between his ears and he watched with terror as the room began stretching and pulsating like Silly Putty in heat. Frito's ears began to grow and his arms changed into badminton rackets. The floor developed holes out of which poured fanged peanut brittle. A score of polka-dotted cockroaches danced a buck-and-wing on his stomach. A Swiss cheese waltzed him twice around the room, and his nose fell off. Frito opened his mouth to speak and a flock of flying earthworms escaped. His gall bladder sang an aria and did a little tap dance on his appendix. He began to lose consciousness, but before it ebbed completely, he heard a six-foot waffle iron giggle, 'If yoo dig it now, jes' wade till th' *rush* hits you!'

III

INDIGESTION AT THE
SIGN OF THE GOODE EATS

The golden brightness of late morning was already warming the grass when Frito finally awoke, his head sore afflicted, and his mouth tasting like the bottom of a birdcage. Looking about, every joint aching, he saw that he and his three still-slumbering companions were at the very edge of the Wood, and before them was the four-lane wagon rut that would lead them directly to Whee! There was no sign of Tim Benzedrine. Frito mused that the events of the previous night might have been the idle dream of a boggie whose tummy writhed full of spoiled potato salad. Then his bloodshot eyes saw the small paper bag resting next to his knapsack, with a scrawled note attached. Curiously, Frito read:

Dere Fritoad,

Two badd yoo copped outt sso sooon lazt nighgt. Missed somm grooovy ttrps. Hoap the rring thinng wurcs outt awrighgth

Peece,
Timm

P.S. Hear ar som outt of sighgt stash which I am laying onn yoo guyys. Mmust sine off as rush iss comcomcoming ohgodohgodohgodohgod$5¢%* @+=!

Frito peeked inside the dirty paper sack and saw a number of colored candy beans, much like the ones they had eaten the night before. *Odd*, thought Frito, *but they may prove useful. Who knows?* Thus, after an hour or so of cajoling his fellows to their senses, Frito and the party tramped off toward Whee rapping much of their adventure the previous evening.

Whee was the chief village of Wheeland, a small and swampy region populated mostly by star-nosed moles and folk who wished that they were somewhere else. The village enjoyed a brief popularity when, through a surveyor's fortuitous hiccup, the four-lane Intershire Turnpath was mistakenly built right through the center of the pathetic little twarf. Then, for a time, the populace lived high on the hog off the proceeds from illegal speed traps, parking violations, and occasional bald-faced hijackings. A small tourist influx from the Sty led to the construction of cheap diners, flimsy souvenir stands, and prefabricated historical landmarks. But the growing cloud of 'troubles' from the east abruptly ended such trade as there was. Instead, a trickle of refugees came from the eastern lands bearing few belongings and fewer smarts.

Not ones to miss an opportunity, the men and boggies of Whee labored together in harmony selling the heavily accented immigrants shorter names and interests in perpetual-motion machines. They also supplemented their purses by hawking black-market visas to the Sty to the few unfortunates who were not familiar with the place.

The men of Whee were stooped, squat, splay-toed, and stupid. Heavily ridged over the eyes and prone to rather poor posture, they were often mistaken for Neanderthals, a common confusion that the latter deeply resented. Slow to anger or pretty much anything else, they lived peacefully with their boggie neighbors, who were themselves tickled pink to find somebody farther down the evolutionary scale.

Together, the two peoples now lived on the few farthings they made off the wetbacks and the dole, a common fruit shaped like your pancreas and about as appetizing.

The village of Whee had some six dozen small houses, most of them built of wax paper and discarded corks. They were arranged in sort of a circle inside the protecting moat, whose stench alone could drop a dragon at a hundred paces.

Pinching their nostrils, the company crossed the creaky drawbridge and read the sign at the gate:

WELCOME TO QUAINT, HISTORICAL WHEE
POPULATION 1,064 ~~388~~ 96 AND STILL GROWING!

Two sleepy-eyed guards bestirred themselves just long
enough to relieve the protesting Spam of his remaining
tablespoons. Frito surrendered half of his magic beans,
which the guards munched with speculation.

The boggies beat it before they took effect and, per
Goodgulf's instructions, headed for the orange-and-
green flashing sign at the center of town. There they
found a gaudy plexiglas and chrome inn, whose
blinking sign portrayed a boar, rampant, devoured by
a mouth, drooling. Beneath it was the name of the inn,
the Goode Eats & Lodging. Passing through the
revolving door, the party signaled the bell clerk,
whose nametag read *Hi! I'm HoJo Hominigritts!* Like the
rest of the staff, he was costumed as a suckling pig with
false sow's ears, tail, and papier-mâché snout.

'Howdy!' drawled the fat boggie. 'Ya'll want a
room?'

'Yes,' said Frito, stealing a glance at his companions.
'We're just in town *for a little vacation*, aren't we,
boys?'

'Vacation,' said Moxie, winking at Frito broadly.

'Just a little vacation,' added Pepsi, nodding his head
like an idiot.

'Ya'll sign here please?' said the clerk through his

fake snout. Frito took the quill chained to the desk and wrote the names ALIAS UNDERCOVER, IVAN GOTTA-SECRET, JOHN DOE-SMITH, and IMA PSEUDONYM.

'Any bags, Mr, uh, Undercover?'

'Only under my eyes,' mumbled Frito, turning toward the dining hall.

'Wal,' chuckled the clerk, 'just leave these here sacks an' I'll *ring* a bellhop.'

'Fine,' said Frito, hurrying away.

'Now y'all have a good time now,' the clerk called after them, 'an' if y'all want anything, just *ring*!'

Out of earshot, Frito turned worriedly to Spam. 'You don't think he *knows* anything,' he whispered, 'do you?'

'Naw, Master Frito,' said Spam, massaging his stomach. 'Let's grab some grub!'

The four entered the dining room and sat at a booth near the roaring propane fireplace that eternally roasted a large cement boar on a motorized spit. The soft notes of a badly played Muzak eddied through the crowded room as the ravenous boggies studied the menu, which was ingeniously shaped like a sow giving birth. As Frito considered an 'Uncle Piggy's Oink-Oink Burger-on-a-Bun' flambéed in purest linseed oil, Spam hungrily ogled the scantily clad 'piglets' who served as waitresses, each buxom wench also outfitted in fake tail, ears, and snout.

One of the piglets sidled up to the table for their order as Spam greedily took stock of her big red eyes, crooked blond wig, and hairy legs.

'Youse slobs wanna order yet?' asked the piglet as she teetered uncomfortably on her spiked heels.

'Two Oink-Oink Burgers and two Bow-Wow Specials, please,' answered Frito respectfully.

'Somethun' t' *ring*, uh, I mean, *drink*, sir?'

'Just four Orca-Colas, thank you.'

'Gotcha.'

As the waitress lurched off, wobbling on her heels and tripping over her long, black scabbard, Frito surveyed the crowd for anyone suspicious. A few boggies, some swarthy-looking men, a drunken troll passed out at the counter. The usual.

Relieved, Frito allowed his three companions to mix with the others, warning them to keep their lips buttoned about the 'you-know-what.' The waitress returned with Frito's burger as Spam traded some pointless anecdotes with a pair of leprechauns in the corner and the twins entertained some seedy-looking gremlins with their cunning pantomime, *The Old Cripple and His Daughters*, a sure-fire hit in the Sty. As growing numbers roared with mirth at their obscene posturings, Frito munched his tasteless burger thoughtfully, wondering what the Great Ring's fate would be when they reached Riv'n'dell, and Goodgulf.

Suddenly, Frito's grinders jammed against a small hard object in the burger. Cursing under his breath, Frito reached into his throbbing mouth and extracted a tiny metal cylinder. Unscrewing the top, he removed a tinier strip of microvellum, on which he made out the words: *Beware! You are in great danger. You are embarked on a long journey. You will soon meet a tall, dark Ranger. You weigh exactly fifty-nine pounds.*

Frito drew in his breath with fright and his eyes sought the sender of this message. At last they came to rest on a tall, dark Ranger seated at the counter, a double root beer untouched before him. The lean figure was dressed entirely in gray, and his eyes were hidden by a black mask. Across his chest were crossed bandoleers of silver bullets, and a pearl-handled broadsword dangled ominously from one lean hip. As if feeling Frito's eyes upon him, he turned slowly on his stool and met them, putting a gloved finger to his lips for secrecy. He then pointed toward the door of the men's room and held out five fingers. FIVE MINUTES. He pointed toward Frito and then to himself. By this time half the patrons had turned to watch, and thinking it was a game of charades, were encouraging him with shouts of 'Famous saying?' and 'Sounds like!'

The young boggie pretended to take no heed of the stranger and reread the note. *Danger*, it said. Frito stared thoughtfully into the sediment of fish hooks and the frothy head of ground glass on his Orca-Cola. Making sure no one was watching, he cautiously took the glass over to the large potted palm nearby, which accepted it and placed it carefully on the floor.

His suspicions now fully aroused, Frito edged from the booth, careful not to disturb the decorative listening tube placed in the center of the plastic floral arrangement. Without being seen, he went into the little boggies' room, there to await the dark stranger.

After he had been waiting a few minutes, several patrons using the facilities began to eye Frito curiously as he leaned against a tiled wall whistling, his hands in his pockets. To allay their further inquiry, Frito turned to the vending machine that hung on the wall. 'Well, well, *well*,' he said in a stage whisper, 'just what I've been looking for!' He then proceeded, with elaborate carelessness, to work the machine with the change in his farthing purse.

Fifteen bird whistles, eight compasses, six miniature lighters, and four packs of nasty little rubber novelties later, a mysterious knocking was heard at the door. Finally one of the patrons hidden by a stall yelled, 'F'cryin' out loud, somebody let the s.o.b. in!' The door swung open and the masked visage of the dark stranger appeared and beckoned Frito around the corner.

'I have a message for you, Mr *Bugger*,' said the stranger.

Frito's burger rose at the sound of his true name.

'But – but I theenk you are meestaken, señor,' began Frito lamely, 'I velly solly but my honorable name not—'

'This message is from Goodgulf the Wizard,' said the stranger, 'if the name by which thee calls thyself answers to the title of *Frito Bugger*!'

'I are,' said Frito, confused and frightened.

'And thee hast the Ring?'

'Maybe I do, and maybe I don't,' countered Frito, stalling for time. The stranger lifted Frito by his narrow lapels.

'*And thee hast the Ring?*'

'Yes, already,' squealed Frito. 'So I've got it! So sue me.'

'Be not afraid, allay thy fears, quail not, and hold thy horses,' laughed the man. 'I am a friend of thine.'

'And you have a message for me from Goodgulf?' gulped Frito, feeling his burger settling a bit. The tall one unzipped a secret compartment in a saddlebag on his shoulder and handed Frito a slip which read:

'Three shorts, four pairs socks, two shirts, chain mail, heavy starch?' Impatiently, the stranger snatched the ancient gag from the boggie's paw and replaced it with a folded parchment. Frito's glance at the Michaelmas Seals and Goodgulf's X-rune imprinted in hardened bubble gum verified the sender.

Hurriedly he tore it open, saving the gum for Spam. For later. With difficulty he deciphered the familiar Palmer Method characters. They read:

Frito-lad,

The halberd has fallen! The fewmets have hit the windmill! Sorhed's Nozdrul have gotten wind of our little dodge and are beating the bush for 'four boggies, one with a pink tail.' Doesn't take any abacus to figure out somebody's spilled the gruel. Get out of wherever you are fast, and don't lose the you-know-what. I'll try to meet you at Wingtip, if not, look me up in Riv'n'dell. In any case, don't take any oaken tuppences. And don't mind Stomper, he's a good egg, ut-bay ot-nay oo-tay ight-bray, if you know what I mean.

                              Must close, left some
                                thing on the Bunsen,

                                      Goodgulf

P.S. How do you like the new stationery? Picked it up for a plainchant at Hambone's Dept!

Once again Frito's Oink-Oink Burger rose to the occasion. Fighting down its untimely reappearance, Frito gasped, 'Then we are not safe here.'

'Have no fear, lowly boggie,' said Stomper, 'for I, Arrowroot of Arrowshirt, am with thee. Goodgulf must have spoken of me in the letter. I have many names—'

'I'm sure you do, Mr Arrowshirt,' Frito broke in, panicking. 'But it's mud and then some if we don't get out of here. I think somebody in this cheap joint wants my scalp, and not for a lanolin massage, either!'

Returning to the booth, Frito found the three boggies still feeding their faces. Ignoring the masked stranger, Spam grinned greasily at Frito. 'Been a-wonderin' where ye ha' gone,' he said. 'Want a bite o' my Bow-Wow?'

Frito's Oink-Oink sought repatriation with Spam's Bow-Wow, but he fought it back and made room for Stomper's long knock-knees under the table. The boggies looked at Stomper with torpid disinterest.

'I didn't be thinkin' it was time for trickin' an' treatin' so soon,' said Spam.

Frito stayed Stomper's wrathful hand. 'Listen,' he said quickly, 'this is Stomper, a friend of Goodgulf's and a friend of ours—'

'And I have many names—' began Stomper.

'And he's got many names, but what we have to do now is—' Frito felt a great hulk looming behind him.

'Youse jerks want t' pay now?' rasped a voice hidden beneath a mass of blond hair and a paper snout.

'Uh, sure,' said Frito, 'now your tip would be, aaah . . .' Suddenly Frito felt a strong, clawed hand reach into his pocket.

'Don't bother, bub,' snarled the voice, 'I'll just *ring this up*! Haw haw haw haw haw!' With a shrill scream, Frito saw the wig fall from the head of the false piglet, revealing the burning red eyes and foul grin of a Nozdrul! As if hypnotized, Frito stared at the huge wraith's slavering leer, noticing that each tooth had been sharpened to a razor point. *Hate to have his dental bills*, he thought. Frito looked around for help as the giant fiend lifted him and rifled his pockets, searching for the Great Ring.

'C'mon, c'mon,' the monster growled, growing impatient, 'Let's have it!' Eight other huge waitresses closed in, each flashing a menacing set of well-honed choppers. Cruelly they held down the three boggies, white with fear. Of Stomper there was nothing to be seen, save a pair of spurred heels shivering under the table.

'Okay, chipmunk, give!' hissed the evil one, drawing his huge black mace. 'I said – *yeeeeowtch*!' cried the Nozdrul in pain, simultaneously letting go of Frito and jumping straight up in the air. From below the table rose a sharp, barbed blade. Stomper leaped up.

'*Oh Dragonbreth! Gilthorpial!*' he yodeled, waving his cleaver around like a madman. He lunged at the nearest wraith with his unwieldy sword. *'Banzai!'* he screamed. *'No quarter asked or given! Damn the torpedoes!'* Taking a vicious swipe, Stomper missed his mark by a good yard and tripped on his scabbard.

The nine stared at the writhing, foaming maniac with round, red eyes. The sight of Stomper filled them with awe. They stood speechless. Suddenly one of the stunned creatures began to titter, then chuckle. Another guffawed. Two more joined in, chortling loudly, and finally all nine were in the throes of hysterical, side-aching laughter. Stomper, puffing and enraged, stood up and tripped on his cape, spilling his silver bullets all over the floor. The whole dining room roared with unbelieving hilarity. Two Nozdrul collapsed to the ground, helplessly giggling. Others staggered about, great red tears rolling down their scaly cheeks, gasping for air and incapable of holding their maces. *Haw haw haw!* Stomper got to his feet, his face beet-red with anger. He lifted his sword, and the blade fell off the handle. *Haw haw haw haw haw!* The Nozdrul rolled and writhed on the ground, clutching their ribs. Stomper replaced the blade, took a mighty wind-up, and firmly embedded the point in the cement pig. *HAW HAW HAW HAW HAW HAW HAW HAW HAW HAW HAW HAW HAW HAW HAW HAW HAW HAW HAW!*

At this point, seeing that no one was paying any

attention to him, Frito picked up one of the heavy, discarded maces and calmly proceeded to beat some heads in. Moxie, Spam, and Pepsi followed his example and went among the gibbering wraiths administering random kicks to groins and breadbaskets.

Finally, the deranged Arrowroot accidentally cut the pulley ropes to the room's main chandelier, simultaneously fixing the wagons of the semiconscious wraiths directly below and plunging the room into total darkness. The boggies dashed blindly for the door, dragging Stomper after them through the temporary blackout. Bobbing and weaving past the glowing eyes, they escaped and ran breathlessly down back alleys and past the snoring guards until they crossed the drawbridge and hit open ground. As Frito ran on he felt the curious eyes of the villagers upon him and his frantic companions. Frito hoped that they would not inform the tools of Sorhed. Thankfully he saw that they took little notice of them and went about their evening chores, lighting signal fires and releasing carrier pigeons.

Once outside the town, Stomper led them into a thick sedge and bade them to be small and quiet lest they be seen by Sorhed's agents, who would soon revive and mount the hunt.

The party was still panting when sharp-eared Arrowroot adjusted the volume on his hearing aid and laid his head to the ground.

'Hark and lo!' he whispered, 'I do hear the sound of Nine Riders galloping nigh the road in full battle array.' A few minutes later a dispirited brace of steers ambled awkwardly past, but to give Stomper his due, they did carry some rather lethal-looking antlerettes.

'The foul Nozdrul have bewitched my ears,' mumbled Stomper as he apologetically replaced his batteries, 'but it is safe to proceed, for the nonce.' It was at that moment that the thundering hooves of the dreaded pig riders echoed along the road. Just in time the company dove back to cover and the vengeful searchers sped past. When the clanking of armor dwindled in the distance, five heads reappeared above the bushes, their teeth chattering like cheap maracas.

' 'Twas a near thing!' said Spam. 'Came nigh to a-spoilin' me pantaloons.'

The party chose to push on toward Wingtip before the sun rose. The moon was swathed in a shawl of heavy cloud as they traveled to the lofty peak, a long finger of granite near the southern base of the legendary Hartz Mountains, scaled by few save an occasional winded guttersnipe.

Stomper walked along in the cool night breeze without speaking, silent except for the faint jingling of his zinc-plated spurs. The twins were fascinated with the pearl-handled sword which he called Krona,

Conqueror of Dozens. Moxie sidled up to the lean masked man.

'That's a neat toadsticker you got there, Mr Arrow-shirt,' said the inquisitive boggie.

'Aye,' said Stomper, quickening his pace a bit.

'Doesn't look like the regular issue. Must be a special model, huh, mister?'

'Aye,' replied the tall man, dilating his nostrils slightly with annoyance.

Quick as a packrat, Moxie snatched the weapon from its holster. 'Okay if I take a look?' Stomper, without batting an eye, let fly with a hand-tooled boot that sent the young boggie bouncing like a jai-alai ball.

'Nay,' snapped Stomper, retrieving his blade.

'I don't think he meant to be rude, Mr Arrowshirt,' said Frito, helping Moxie to his archless feet. There followed an embarrassed silence. Spam, whose knowledge of warfare was limited to childhood torturing of the family pullets, nevertheless began to sing a snatch of song he had once learned:

> *Barbisol was Twodor's king*
> *Whose foes his mighty blade did sting,*
> *Till one day it got all rusted,*
> *And Sorhed's parry left it busted.*

Then, to the boggie's surprise, a fat tear fell from Stomper's eye and his voice sobbed in the darkness:

> *Thus gloried Twodor came to nothing,*
> *Out of the king was beat the stuffing.*
> *And thus we live in fear of Fordor*
> *Till Krona's back in working order!*

The boggies gasped and looked at their companion as if for the first time. With recognition they recognized the legendary weak chin and buck teeth of Barbisol's descendant.

'Then you must be the rightful King of Twodor!' cried Frito.

The tall Ranger looked at them impassively.

'These things you say may be affirmed,' he said, 'but I do not wish to make a statement at this time, for there is another, oft-forgotten verse to this sad and doleful song:

> *Against the True King Sorhed's workin'*
> *So play your cards close to your jerkin,*
> *For fortune strums a mournful tune*
> *For those whose campaigns peak too soon.'*

Watching the newly revealed ruler trudge on in his lowly garb, the young Frito grew again thoughtful and pondered long on the many ironies of life.

As the sun's rim broke on the far horizon its first tentative rays illuminated Wingtip. After an hour of strenuous climbing they reached the top and rested gratefully on the flat granite apex, while Stomper scrounged around for some sign of Goodgulf. Nosing about a large gray rock, Stomper stopped and called to Frito. Frito looked at the stone and discerned the crude skull-and-bones etched into its surface, and with it the X-rune of the Old Wizard.

'Goodgulf has passed this way recently,' said Stomper, 'and unless I read these runes awrong, he means this place as a secure camp for us.'

Nevertheless Frito bedded down with nagging misgivings. *But*, he reminded himself, *he is a king, and all*. The bridge across the Gallowine and the way to Riv'n'dell were only a short distance; there they would be safe from the marauding Swine Riders. Sleep was now long overdue, and he sighed with pleasure as he curled up under a low shelf of stone. Soon he was falling fast asleep, lulled by the soft *snuffling* noises and the clanking of armor below.

'Awake! Awake! Fiends! Foes! *Flee!*' someone was whispering, waking Frito from his dreams. Stomper's hand jostled him roughly. Obeying him, Frito peered down the slope and made out nine black forms inching stealthily up the mountain toward their hiding place.

'It seemeth that I read the signs awrong,' muttered the perplexed guide. 'Soon they will be upon us unless we divert their wrath.'

'How?' asked Pepsi.

'Yes, how?' joined in Guess Who.

Stomper looked at the boggies. 'One of the party must stay behind to delay them while we dash for the bridge.'

'But who——?'

'Never fear,' said Stomper quickly. 'I have here in my gauntlet four lots, three long and a short for him we throw to the – er – for he who will have his name emblazoned in the pantheon of heroes.'

'Four?' said Spam. 'What about *you*?'

The Ranger straightened with great dignity. 'Surely,' he said, 'you would not wish me an unfair advantage seeing that it was I who made up the lots?'

Mollified, the boggies drew the pipe cleaners. Spam drew the short.

'Two out of three?' he whined. But his fellows had already disappeared over the lip of the peak and were racing down as fast as they could. Panting and puffing, a fat tear rolled from Frito's eye. He would miss him.

Spam looked down the opposite slope and saw the dismounted Nozdrul picking their way toward him quickly. Crouching behind a rock, he screamed courageously at them. 'If I were ye,' he called, 'I'd not come any closer! Ye'll be sorry if ye do!' Unheeding, the fierce knights drew even nearer. 'You're really a-goin' t' get it!' yelled Spam rather unconvincingly. Still the Riders grew nearer, and Spam lost his nerve. Taking out his white handkerchief, he waved it about and pointed toward his retreating friends. 'Don't be wastin' your time with me,' he cried. 'The one with the Ring is high-tailin' it thataway!'

Hearing this from below, Frito winced and pumped his fat legs harder. Stomper's long and gimpy shanks had already brought him across the bridge and onto the safety of the other bank, the neutral territory of the elves. Frito looked behind him. He wouldn't make it in time!

Stomper watched the deadly race from the cover of some briars on the bank of the stream.

'Hie thee faster,' he called helpfully, 'for the evil ones are right behind thee!' Then he hid his eyes.

The rumble of pigs' feet grew louder and louder in Frito's ears, and he could hear the lethal *swish* of their horrible Nozdrulville Sluggers. He made a last, desperate burst of speed, but tripped and skidded to a stop only a few feet from the border. Cackling with evil amusement, the nine surrounded Frito, their squint-eyed steeds grunting for Frito's blood.

'Blood! Blood!' they grunted.

Frito looked up, terrified, and saw them as they slowly closed the ring, only an arm's length from death. The leader of the pack, a tall beefy wraith with chrome-plated greaves, laughed savagely and raised his mace.

'Hee hee hee, filthy rodent! Now is the time for fun!'

Frito cowered. 'Maybe it is, and maybe it isn't,' he said, pulling his favorite bluff.

'Arrrgh!' screamed an impatient Nozdrul, who, by coincidence, happened to be named Argh. 'C'mon, let's cream this little creep! The boss said take his Ring and croak him then 'n' there!'

Frito's mind raced. He decided to play his last card.

'Well dat's sho' nuff fine wit me, 'cause ah sho' doan wan' you t' do the bad thing to' po' li'l me!' said Frito, bugging out his eyes and rolling them like ball bearings.

'Har har har!' chortled another Rider. 'What can *you* think of that's worse than what we're *gonna* do with ya?' The fiends drew closer to hear the terrible fear Frito harbored in his breast.

The boggie whistled and pretended to play the banjo. He then sang a verse of 'Ole Man Ribber' as he ambled back and forth on shuffling feet, scratched his woolly head, and danced a cakewalk while picking watermelon seeds from his ears, all with natural rhythm.

'Sure can dance,' muttered one of the Riders.

'Sure gonna *die*!' screamed another, thirsting for Frito's throat.

'*Sho'* I gwine t' die,' drawled Frito. 'Yo' kin do mos' anythin' t' po' li'l me, Br'er Nozdrul, so long as yo' *please doan throw me in dat briar patch ober dere!*'

At this all the sadistic Riders sniggered.

'If that's what you're scared of most,' bellowed a voice full of malice, 'then *that's what we'll do to you*, ya little jerk!'

Frito felt himself lifted by a horny black hand and flung far over the Gallowine and into the scrubby bush on the other side. Gleefully, he stood up and fished out the Ring, making sure it still hung on his chain.

But the crafty Riders were not long deceived by Frito's ruse. They spurred their drooling swine to the bridge, intent on recapturing the boggie and his precious Ring. But, as Frito saw with surprise, the Black Nine were halted at the foot of the crossing by a figure robed in shining raiment.

'Toll, please,' commanded the figure of the startled Riders. The pursuers were again dumbfounded when they were directed to a hastily lettered sign tacked to a support:

Elfboro Municipal Toll Bridge
Single Wayfarers . . . . . . 1 farthing
Double-axled Haywains . . . . . 2 farthings
Black Riders . . . . 45 gold pieces

'Let us cross!' snapped an angry Nozdrul.

'Certainly,' replied the attendant pleasantly. 'Now let's see, there's one, two . . . ah, *nine* of you at forty-five apiece, that makes . . . uuuuhh, four hundred and five beans, exactly, please. In cash.'

Hurriedly, the Nozdrul searched their saddlebags as their leader cursed angrily and shook his slugger with frustration.

'Listen,' he stormed, 'what kind of dough do you think we make, anyhow? Ain't there some sorta discount for civil servants?'

'I'm sorry—' smiled the attendant.

'How 'bout a Wayfarer's Letter of Credit? They're as good as bullion anywhere.'

'Sorry, this is a bridge, not a countinghouse,' replied the figure impassively.

'My personal check? It's backed up by the treasure rooms of Fordor.'

'No money, no crossee, friend.'

The Nozdruls quivered with rage, but turned their mounts around, preparing to ride off. Before they left, however, the leader shook a gnarled fist.

'This ain't the end of this, punk! You'll hear from us again!'

Saying this, the nine spurred their farting porkers and sped away in a great cloud of dust and dung.

Observing this near impossible escape from certain death, Frito wondered how much longer the authors were going to get away with such tripe. He wasn't the only one.

Stomper and the other boggies ran to Frito, extending their congratulations on his escape. They then drew close to the mysterious figure, who approached and, espying Stomper among them, raised his hands in greeting and sang:

> *O NASA O UCLA! O Etaion Shrdlu!*
> *O Escrow Beryllium! Pandit J. Nehru!*

Stomper raised his hands and answered, '*Shantih Billerica!*' They met and embraced, exchanging words of friendship and giving the secret handshake.

The boggies studied the stranger with interest. He introduced himself as Garfinkel of the elves. When he had shed himself of his robes, the boggies regarded with curiosity his ring-encrusted hands, his open-collared Ban-Lon tunic, and his silver beach clogs.

'Thought you would have been here days ago,' said the balding elf. 'Any trouble along the way?'

'I could write a book,' said Frito prophetically.

'Well,' said Garfinkel, 'we'd better make tracks before those B-movie heavies return. They may be stupid, but they sure can be persistent.'

'So new?' muttered Frito, who found himself muttering more and more lately.

The elf looked doubtfully at the boggies. 'You guys

know how to ride?' Without waiting for an answer he whistled loudly through his gold teeth. A clump of high sedge rustled and several overweight merino sheep bounded into view, bleating irritably.

'Mount up,' said Garfinkel.

Frito, more or less athwart an unpromising ungulant, rode last in the procession away from the Gallowine toward Riv'n'dell. He slipped his hand into his pocket, found the Ring, and took it out in the fading light. Already it was beginning to work its slow change upon him, the transformation of which Dildo had warned. He was constipated.

IV

FINDERS KEEPERS,
FINDERS WEEPERS

After three days of hard riding that had put many a furlong between them and the Black Riders, the weary boggies came at last to the low kneehills which surrounded the valley of Riv'n'dell with a natural wall that protected it from occasional marauders too stupid or small to scale the sheer knolls and mounds. But their sure-footed mounts easily overcame these obstacles with short, heart-stopping hops, and in no time Frito and his companions had reached the summit of the last hillock and looked down on the orange roofs and cupolas of the elfish ranchellas. Urging on their panting ruminants, they galloped down the winding corduroy road that led to the dwellings of Orlon.

It was late in the gray fall afternoon when the procession of sheepback riders rode into Riv'n'dell, led by Garfinkel astride his magnificent woolly stallion, Anthrax. An ill wind was blowing, and granite hailstones were falling from brooding clouds. As the party drew rein in front of the main lodge, a tall elf robed in finest percale and wearing bucks of blinding whiteness stepped onto the porch and greeted them.

'Welcome to the Last Homely House East of the Sea and Gift Shoppe,' he said. 'Barca-Loungers in every room.'

Garfinkel and the tall elf thumbed their noses in the ancient salute of their race and exchanged greetings in elvish. 'A syanon esso decca hi hawaya,' said Garfinkel, lightly springing from his animal.

'O movado silvathin nytol niceta-seeya,' replied the tall elf; then turning to Stomper he said: 'I am Orlon.'

'Arrowroot son of Arrowshirt, at your service,' said Stomper, dismounting clumsily.

'And these?' said Orlon, pointing to the four boggies asleep on their dormant mounts.

'Frito and his companions, boggies from the Sty,' said Stomper. At the mention of his name, Frito gurgled loudly and fell off his sheep, and the Ring dropped out of his clothes, and rolled to Orlon's feet. One of the sheep trotted up, licked it, and turned into a fire hydrant.

'Oog,' mumbled Orlon, and staggered inside. Garfinkel followed him into the little building, and a stream of low elvish followed. Arrowroot stood listening for a moment, then went around to Spam, Moxie, and Pepsi and woke them up with a series of finger jabs and pivot-kicks. Frito retrieved the Ring and slipped it into his pocket. 'So this is Riv'n'dell,' he said, rubbing his eyes with wonder as he looked at the strange elvish houses of prestressed gingerbread and ferrocandy.

'Look, Master Frito,' said Spam, pointing up the road. 'Elfs, lots of 'em. Ooooo, I must be dreaming. I wish the old Fatlip could see me now.'

'I wish I were dead,' whined Pepsi.

'So do I,' said Moxie.

'May the good fairy what sits in the sky grant yer ev'ry wish,' said Spam.

'Where is Goodgulf, I wonder,' wondered Frito.

Garfinkel strode back out onto the porch and produced a small tin whistle on which he blew a single, ear-splitting, flat note, whereupon the sheep wandered aimlessly away.

'Magical,' sighed Spam.

'Follow me,' said Garfinkel, and he led Stomper and the boggies along a narrow muddy path which wound through clumps of flowering rhodogravure bushes and towering shoe trees. As he walked along, Frito smelled an evanescent fragrance of new-mown hay mingled with bleach and mustard, and from afar off he heard the delicate, heart-breaking twangs of a mouth-harp and a few shreds of an elvish song:

> *Row, row, row your elebethiel saliva githiel*
> *Mann a fubar lothario syzygy snafu*
> *O bring back my sucaryl Penna Ariz Fla mass.*

At the end of the path stood a small bungalow made of polished Joyvah Halvah and surrounded by a bed of glass flowers. Garfinkel turned the door's all-day sucker and motioned the party inside. They found themselves in a large room which entirely filled the little house. There were a great many beds arranged around the walls, all of which looked as though they had been recently slept in by perverted kangaroos, and in the corners were a few odd chairs and tables which showed quite clearly the hand, and foot, of the elvish craftsmen. In the center of the room was a large table littered with the remnants of a violent game of three-pack canasta and several bowls of artificial fruit which couldn't have been mistaken for the real thing at fifty meters. These Moxie and Pepsi immediately ate.

'Make yourself at home,' said Garfinkel, as he left. 'Check-out time is three o'clock.'

Stomper slumped heavily into a chair, which folded up under him with a muffled crack.

Garfinkel was not gone more than five minutes when there came a knock at the door, and Spam went, rather irritably, to answer it. 'It had better be food,' he mumbled, 'cause I'm gonna eat it.'

He opened the door with a jerk, revealing a mysterious stranger in a long gray cape and hood, wearing thick, black eyeglasses with a false rubber nose quite unconvincingly dangling from the bridge. The dark figure had a cardboard mustache, a dustmop wig, and a huge, handpainted tie with a picture of an elf-maiden. In his left hand was a mashie-niblick, and on his feet he wore shower clogs. He was puffing a fat cigar.

Spam reeled back in astonishment, and Stomper, Moxie, Pepsi, and Frito cried in unison, 'Goodgulf!'

The old man shuffled in, discarding his disguises to reveal the familiar faith healer and bunco artist. 'Lo, it is I,' admitted the Wizard, dispiritedly plucking a few strings out of his hair. With that he went around and shook all their hands very hard, shocking them with the little electric buzzer he invariably carried concealed in his palm.

'Well, well,' said Goodgulf, 'here we all are again.'

'I'd sooner be in a dragon's colon,' said Frito.

'I trust you still have *it*,' said Goodgulf, eyeing Frito.

'Do you mean the Ring?'

'Silence,' commanded Goodgulf in a loud voice. 'Speak not of the Great Ring here or anywhere. If Sorhed's spies discovered that you, Frito Bugger, hailing from the Sty, had the One Ring, all would be lost. And his spies are everywhere. The Nine Black Riders are abroad again, and there are those who claim to have seen the Seven Santinis, the Six Danger Signs, and the entire Trapp family, including the dog. Even the walls have ears,' he said, pointing to two huge lobes which were protruding from behind the mantelpiece.

'Is there no hope?' gasped Frito. 'Is nowhere safe?'

'Who can know?' said Goodgulf, and a shadow seemed to pass over his face. 'I would say more,' he said, 'but a shadow seems to have passed over my face,' and with that he fell strangely silent.

Frito began to weep, and Stomper leaned forward, and putting his hand reassuringly on Frito's shoulder, said, 'Fear not, dear boggie, I will be with you all the way, no matter what may befall.'

'Same here,' said Spam, and fell asleep.

'Us too,' said Moxie and Pepsi, yawning.

Frito remained inconsolable.

When the boggies awoke from their nap, Goodgulf and Stomper were gone, and the moon was shining fuzzily through the taffy windows. They had finished eating the curtains and were starting in on the lampshades when Garfinkel returned, clad in finest cheesecloth, and led them down to the lodge building they had seen when they first arrived. It was large and brightly lit, and the night was filled with the brouhaha from within. As they approached, there came a silence, and then the plaintive, blackboard-scraping shriek of a nose-flute pierced the air.

'They're giving a pig a rough time of it in there,' said Spam, blocking his ears.

'Hush,' said Frito, and a voice rose in song, filling the boggies with a vague sense of nausea.

> *A Unicef clearasil*
> *Gibberish 'n' drivel*
> *O Mennen mylar muriel*
> *With a hey derry tum gardol*
> *O Yuban necco glamorene?*
> *Enden nytol, vaseline!*
> *Sing hey nonny nembutal.*

With a last twittering wail, the music died away, and half a dozen stunned birds plopped heavily to the ground in front of Frito.

'What was that?' asked Frito.

'It is an ancient lament in the tongue of the Auld Elves,' sighed Garfinkel. 'It tells of Unicef and his long and bitter search for a clean rest room. "Are there no facilities here?" he cries. "Is there no washroom?" No one seems to know.'

So said Garfinkel and led the boggies into the House of Orlon. They found themselves in a long, high-raftered hall down the center of which ran an endless table. At one end was a huge oak mantelpiece and from high above hung brass chandeliers in which fine ear-wax candles spluttered brightly. Along the table sat the usual flotsam and jetsam of Lower Middle Earth; elves, fairies, Martians, several frogs, dwarves, gnomes, a few token men, a handful of bugbears, several trolls wearing sunglasses, a couple of goblins the Christian Scientists had worked over, and a dragon who had gotten fed up.

At the head of the table sat Orlon and the Lady Lycra robed in cloth of dazzling whiteness and brightness. Dead they looked, and yet it was not so, for Frito could see their eyes shining like wet mushrooms. Bleached was their hair so that it shone like goldenrod, and their faces were as bright and fair as the surface of the moon. All about them zircons, garnets, and lodestones flashed like stars. On their heads were silken lampshades and on their brows were written many things, both fair and foul, such as 'Unleash Chiang Kai-shek' and 'I love my wife but oh you kid.' Asleep they were.

To the left of Orlon sat Goodgulf in a red fez, revealed as a 32nd Degree Mason and Honorary Shriner, and to his right sat Stomper, clad in the white Gene Autry suit of a Ranger. Frito was shown to a seat about halfway down the table between an unusually deformed dwarf and an elf who smelled like a birdnest, and Moxie and Pepsi were sent to a small table in a corner with the Easter Bunny and a couple of tooth fairies.

As with most mythical creatures who live in enchanted forests with no visible means of support, the elves ate rather frugally, and Frito was a little disappointed to find heaped on his plate a small mound of ground nuts, bark, and dirt. Nevertheless, like all boggies, he was capable of eating anything he could Indian-wrestle down his throat and rather preferred dishes that didn't struggle too much, since even a half-cooked mouse can usually beat a boggie two falls out of three. No sooner had he finished eating than the dwarf sitting to his right turned to him and proffered an extremely scaly hand in greeting. *It's at the end of his arm*, thought Frito, nervously shaking it, *it's got to be a hand*.

'Gimlet, son of Groin, your obedient servant,' said the dwarf, bowing to reveal a hunchback. 'May you always buy cheap and sell dear.'

'Frito, son of Dildo, yours,' said Frito in some confusion, racking his brains for the correct reply. 'May your hemorrhoids shrink without surgery.'

The dwarf looked puzzled but not displeased. 'Then you are the boggie of whom Goodgulf spoke, the Ringer?'

Frito nodded.

'Do you have *it* with you?'

'Would you like to see it?' asked Frito politely.

'Oh, no thanks,' said Gimlet, 'I had an uncle who had a magic tieclip and one time he sneezed and his nose fell off.'

Frito nervously touched a nostril.

'Excuse the interruption,' said the elf on his left, spitting accurately into the dwarf's left eye, 'but I couldn't help overhearing your conversation with Gabby Hayes. Are you in fact the boggie with the bijou?'

'I am,' said Frito and sneezed violently.

'Allow me,' said the elf, proffering Gimlet's beard to Frito, who was by now sneezing uncontrollably. 'I am Legolam, of the Elves of Northern Weldwood.'

'Elf-dog,' hissed Gimlet, retrieving his beard.

'Pig of a dwarf,' suggested Legolam.

'Toymaker.'

'Gold digger.'

'Flit.'

'Wart.'

'Would you like to hear a joke or a song or something?' said Frito, becoming alarmed. 'It seems there was this wandering dragon, and he comes to this farmhouse and the farmer—'

'A song,' agreed Gimlet and Legolam.

'Of course,' said Frito, and desperately trying to recall some of Dildo's doggerel, he began to sing in a squeaky voice:

> A King of Elves there was of old,
>   Saranrap by name,
> Who slew the Narcs at Mellowmarsh
>   And Sorhed's host did tame.

And with him marched the stubby dwarves
    Drafted from their mines,
But when the fearsome Battle raged
    They hid behind the lines.

    Sing: Clearasil, metrecal, lavoris in chorus
    They hid behind the lines!

Angered was the mighty King
    About to raise the dickens,
'Just let me get my hands,' quoth he,
    'On those half-pint chickens!'

Fearful were the chicken-Dwarves,
    But mickle crafty too,
King Yellowbac, their skins to save,
    The elves did try to woo.

    Sing: Twist-a-cap, reynoldswrap, gardol and duz
    The elves he tried to woo!

'If you doubt our loyalty,'
    Yello told the King,
'Take this gift, a dwarfish sword
    That packs a mighty sting.

'Clearasil, it's called by name,'
    The clever Dwarf spoke on,
'Take this bribe, and let us let
    Bygones be bygone.'

Sing: Cadillac, pickapack, Edsel and coke
Bygones be bygone.

'*I accept this wondrous gift,*
 And think you Dwarves are tops,'
Said he, as he took the sword
 And smote him in the chops.

And since that day it's said by all
 In ballad, lay and poem,
'*Only trust an elf or dwarf*
 As far as you can throw 'em!'

 Sing: Oxydol, geritol, wheaties and Trix.
 As far as you can throw 'em!

Just as Frito finished, Orlon suddenly roused himself and signaled for silence. 'Bingo in the Elf Lounge,' he said, and the feast ended.

Frito was making his way to the table where Moxie and Pepsi were sitting when a bony hand reached out of a potted palm and grasped his shoulder. 'Come with me,' said Goodgulf, brushing a frond aside, and led the surprised boggie down the hall and into a small room almost entirely filled by a huge glass-topped table. Orlon and Stomper had already taken seats and as he and Goodgulf sat down Frito was amazed to see his dinner companions, Gimlet and Legolam, enter and seat themselves on opposite sides of the table. They were quickly followed by a heavyset man in iridescent pegged trousers and sharply pointed shoes. Last of all came a small figure in a loud shirt smoking a foul elvish cigar and carrying a Scrabble board.

'Dildo!' cried Frito.

'Ah, Frito my lad,' said Dildo, slapping Frito heavily on the back, 'so you made it after all. Well, well, well.' Orlon held out a moist palm, and Dildo rummaged in his pockets and pulled out a wad of crumpled bills.

'Two, wasn't it?' he said.

'Ten,' said Orlon.

'So it was, so it was,' said Dildo, and dropped the bills in the elf's hand.

'It's been so long since the party,' said Frito. 'What have you been doing?'

'Not much,' said the old boggie. 'A little Scrabble, a little pederasty. I'm retired, you see.'

'But what is this all about? Who are the Black Riders, and what do they want with me? And what has the Ring got to do with it?'

'Much and little, more or less, dear boggie,' explained Orlon. 'But all in good time. This Great Caucus has been called to answer such questions and others, but for now I will say only that there are a-many things amiss afoot, alas.'

'No lie,' said Goodgulf gravely. 'The Nameless No-No is spreading again, and the time has come to act. Frito, the Ring.'

Frito nodded and drew from his pocket the paper-clip chain, link by link. With a short toss, he threw the fatal trinket onto the table, where it landed with a tinny jing.

Orlon gasped. 'The Magic Dingus,' he cried.

'What proof is there that this is the Ring?' asked the man with the pointed shoes.

'There are many signs which can be read by the wise, Bromosel,' announced the Wizard. 'The compass, the whistle, the magic decoder – they're all here. And there is the inscription:

> *Grundig blaupunkt luger frug*
> *Watusi snarf wazoo!*
> *Nixon dirksen nasahist*
> *Rebozo boogaloo.*

Goodgulf's voice had become harsh and distant. An ominous black cloud filled the room. Frito gagged on the thick oily smoke.

'Was that necessary?' asked Legolam, kicking the Wizard's still-belching smoke grenade out the door.

'Rings go better with hocus-pocus,' replied Goodgulf imperiously.

'But what does that mean?' asked Bromosel, rather

annoyed that he was being referred to in the dialogue as 'the man with the pointed shoes.'

'There are many interpretations,' explained Good-gulf. 'My guess is that it's either "The quick brown fox jumped over the lazy dog" or "Don't tread on me."'

No one spoke, and the room fell strangely silent.

Finally Bromosel rose and addressed the Caucus. 'Much is now clear,' he said. 'I had a dream one night in Minas Troney in which seven cows ate seven bushels of wheat, and when they were finished they climbed a red tower and threw up three times, chanting, "Say it now and say it loud, I'm a cow and I'm proud." And then a figure robed in white and bearing a pair of scales came forward and read from a little slip of paper:

> *Five-eleven's your height, one-ninety your weight*
> *You cash in your chips around page eighty-eight.*

'This is grave,' said Orlon.

'Well,' said Stomper, 'I guess it's time we all laid our cards on the table,' and with that he noisily emptied the contents of a faded duffel into a heap in front of him. When he was finished, there was a large pile of odd objects, including a broken sword, a golden arm, a snowflake paperweight, the Holy Grail, the Golden Fleece, the Robe, a piece of the True Cross, and a glass slipper.

'Arrowroot, son of Arrowshirt, heir of Barbisol and King of Minas Troney, at your service,' he said, rather loudly.

Bromosel looked up to the top of the page and winced. 'At least another chapter to go,' he groaned.

'Then the Ring is yours,' cried Frito, and eagerly tossed it into Arrowroot's hat.

'Well, not exactly,' said Arrowroot, dangling the band at the end of its long chain. 'Since it's got magic powers, it belongs to someone more in the mumbo-jumbo, presto-changeo line. To wit, a wizard, for example,' and he neatly slipped the Ring over the end of Goodgulf's wand.

'Ah, yes, verily, in truth,' said Goodgulf quickly. 'That is to say, yes and no. Or perhaps just plain no. As any fool can see, it's a clear case of habeas corpus or tibia fibia, since although this particular gizmo was the work of a wizard – Sorhed, to be exact – this sort of thing was invented by elves, and he was only working under a license, you might say.'

Orlon held the Ring in his hand as if it were an annoyed tarantula. 'Nay,' he said, gravely, 'I cannot claim this great prize, for it is said, "Finders keepers, losers weepers," ' and brushing away an invisible tear, he looped the chain around Dildo's neck.

'And "Let dogs lie if they are sleepers," ' said Dildo, and slipped it into Frito's pocket.

'Then it is settled,' intoned Orlon. 'Frito Bugger shall keep the Ring.'

'Bugger?' said Legolam. 'Bugger? That's curious. There was a nasty little clown named Goddam sniffing around Weldwood on hands and knees looking for a Mr Bugger. It was a little queer.'

'Odd,' said Gimlet. 'A pack of black giants riding huge pigs came through the mountains last month hunting for a boggie named Bugger. Never gave it a second thought.'

'This, too, is grave,' declared Orlon. 'It is only a matter of time before they come here,' he said, pulling a shawl over his head and making a gesture of throwing something of a conciliatory nature to a shark, 'and as neutrals, we would have no choice . . .'

Frito shuddered.

'The Ring and its bearer must go hence,' agreed Goodgulf, 'but where? Who shall guard it?'

'The elves,' said Gimlet.

'The dwarves,' said Legolam.

'The wizards,' said Arrowroot.

'The Men of Twodor,' said Goodgulf.

'That leaves only Fordor,' said Orlon. 'But even a retarded troll would not go there.'

'Even a dwarf,' admitted Legolam.

Frito suddenly felt that all eyes were on him.

'Couldn't we just drop it down a storm drain, or pawn it and swallow the ticket?' he said.

'Alas,' said Goodgulf solemnly, 'it is not that easy.'

'But why?'

'Alas,' explained Goodgulf.

'Alackaday,' Orlon agreed.

'But fear not, dear boggie,' continued Orlon, 'you shall not go alone.'

'Good old Gimlet will go with you,' said Legolam.

'And fearless Legolam,' said Gimlet.

'And noble King Arrowroot,' said Bromosel.

'And faithful Bromosel,' said Arrowroot.

'And Moxie, Pepsi, and Spam,' said Dildo.

'And Goodgulf Grayteeth,' added Orlon.

'Indeed,' said Goodgulf, glaring at Orlon, and if looks could maim, the old elf would have left in a basket.

'So be it. You shall leave when the omens are right,' said Orlon, consulting a pocket horoscope, 'and unless I'm very much mistaken, they will be unmatched in half an hour.'

Frito groaned. 'I wish I had never been born,' he said.

'Do not say that, dear Frito,' cried Orlon. 'It was a happy minute for us all when you were born.'

*

'Well, I guess it's goodbye,' said Dildo, taking Frito aside as they left the caucus room. 'Or should I say "until we meet again"? No, I think goodbye sums it up quite nicely.'

'Goodbye, Dildo,' Frito said, stifling a sob. 'I wish you were coming with us.'

'Ah, yes. But I'm too old for that sort of thing now,' said the old boggie, feigning a state of total paraplegia. 'Anyway, I have a few small gifts for you,' and he produced a lumpy parcel, which Frito opened some-what unenthusiastically in view of Dildo's previous going-away present. But the package contained only a short, Revereware sword, a bulletproof vest full of moth holes, and several well-thumbed novellas with titles like *Elf Lust* and *Goblin Girl*.

'Farewell, Frito,' said Dildo, managing a very con-vincing epileptic fit. 'It's in your hands now, gasp, rattle, o lie me under the greenwood tree, ooooo. Ooog.'

'Farewell, Dildo,' said Frito, and with a last wave went out to join the company. As soon as he had disappeared, Dildo sprang lightly to his feet, and skipped into the hall humming a little song:

> *I sit on the floor and pick my nose*
> *   and think of dirty things*
> *Of deviant dwarfs who suck their toes*
> *   and elves who drub their dings.*

I sit on the floor and pick my nose
and dream exotic dreams
Of dragons who dress in rubber clothes
and trolls who do it in teams.

I sit on the floor and pick my nose
and wish for a thrill or two
For a goblin who goes in for a few no-nos
Or an orc with a thing about glue.

And all of the while I sit and pick
I think of such jolly things
Of whips and screws and leather slacks
Of frottages and stings.

'I grieve to see you leave so soon,' said Orlon quickly, as the company stood assembled around their pack sheep some twenty minutes later. 'But the Shadow is growing and your journey is long. It is best to begin at once, in the night. The Enemy has eyes everywhere.' As he spoke, a large, hair-covered eyeball rolled ominously from its perch in a tree and fell to the ground with a heavy squelch.

Arrowroot drew Krona, the Sword that was broken, now hastily reglued, and waved it over his head. 'Onward,' he cried, 'on to Fordor!'

'Farewell, farewell,' said Orlon impatiently.

'Excelsior,' cried Bromosel, blowing a fierce blast on his duck whistle.

'Sayonara,' said Orlon. 'Aloha. Avaunt. Arroint.'

'Kodak khaki no-doz,' Gimlet cried.

'A dristan nasograph,' shouted Legolam.

'Habeas corpus,' said Goodgulf, waving his wand.

'I have to go poo-poo,' said Pepsi.

'So do I,' said Moxie.

'I'd like ta poo-poo the both o' ye,' said Spam, reaching for a rock.

'Let's go,' said Frito, and the party set off down the road from Riv'n'dell at a walk. In a few short hours they had put several hundred feet between them and the lodge where Orlon still stood, wreathed in smiles. As the party passed over the first slight rise, Frito turned around and looked back over Riv'n'dell. Somewhere in the black distance lay the Sty, and he felt a great longing to return, as a dog might on recalling a long-forgotten spew.

As he watched, the moon rose, there was a meteor shower and a display of the aurora borealis, a cock crowed thrice, it thundered, a flock of geese flew by in the shape of a swastika, and a giant hand wrote *Mene, mene, what's it to you?* across the sky in giant silver letters. Suddenly Frito had the overpowering feeling that he had come to a turning point, that an old chapter in his life was ending and a new one beginning. 'Mush, you brute,' he said, kicking the pack animal in the kidneys, and as the great quadruped staggered forward, tailfirst into the black East, there came from deep in the surrounding forest the sound of some great bird being briefly, but noisily, ill.

V

SOME MONSTERS

For many days the company traveled south, trusting to the eyes of the Ranger, Arrowroot, the keen ears of the boggies, and the wisdom of Goodgulf to lead them. A fortnight after their departure they arrived at a great crossroads and halted to determine the best way to cross the towering Mealey Mountains.

Arrowroot squinted into the distance. 'Behold the grim Mount Badass,' he said, pointing to a large milestone a hundred yards down the road.

'Then we must head east,' said Goodgulf, gesturing with his wand to where the sun was setting redly in a mass of sea-clouds.

A duck flew over quacking loudly. 'Wolves,' cried Pepsi, straining to hear the fading sound.

'It is best that we make camp here tonight,' said Arrowroot, dropping his pack heavily to the ground, where it crushed a hooded cobra. 'Tomorrow we must seek the high pass across the mountains.'

A few minutes later the company sat in the middle of the crossroads around a bright fire over which one of Goodgulf's stage rabbits was merrily roasting. 'A proper fire at last, and no mistake,' said Spam, tossing a rattlesnake on the cheery blaze. 'I reckon none o' Master Pepsi's wolves is likeable to bother us tonight.'

Pepsi snorted. 'A wolf would have to be pretty hard up to eat a road apple like you,' he said, flicking a rock at Spam, which missed him by feet and stunned a puma. Circling far overhead, unseen by the company, the leader of a band of black spy-crows peered through a pair of binoculars, cursed in the harsh tongue of his kind, and swore off grapes for the rest of his life.

'Where are we, and where are we going?' asked Frito.

'We are at a great crossroads,' answered the Wizard, and producing a battered sextant from within his robes, he took sightings on the moon, Arrowroot's cowboy hat, and Gimlet's upper lip. 'Soon we will cross a mountain or a river and pass into another land,' he said.

Arrowroot strode over to Frito. 'Do not fear,' he said, sitting on a wolf, 'we will guide you safely through.'

The next day dawned clear and bright, as is so often the case when it does not rain, and the spirits of the company were considerably raised. After a frugal breakfast of milk and honey, they set out in single file behind Arrowroot and Goodgulf, with Spam bringing up the rear behind the pack sheep, toward whom he expressed a boggie's usual fondness for fuzzy animals.

'Oh, for some mint sauce,' he lamented.

The party traveled many leagues* along the broad, well-paved highway that led east to the odorous feet of the Mealey Mountains, and later in the afternoon they came to the first of the low kneehills. There the road quickly disappeared in a mass of rubble and the ruins of an ancient toll booth. Beyond, a short, steep valley as black as coal stretched ominously to the rocky slope of the mountains. Arrowroot signaled for a halt, and the company gathered to look at the forbidding landscape.

'This is an evil place, I fear,' said Arrowroot, slipping on the sticky black paint which covered every inch of the land.

'It is the Black Valley,' said Goodgulf solemnly.

'Are we in Fordor already?' asked Frito hopefully.

'Do not mention that black land in this black land,' said the Wizard darkly. 'No, it is not Fordor, but it seems that it has been touched by the Enemy of all Right-Thinking Folk.'

As they stood looking over the dreary vale, there came the howl of wolves, the roar of bears, and the cry of vultures.

'It's quiet,' said Gimlet.

* A league is approximately 3 furlongs or only a knot short of a hectare.

'Too quiet,' said Legolam.

'We cannot stay here,' said Arrowroot.

'No,' agreed Bromosel, looking across the gray surface of the page to the thick half of the book still in the reader's right hand. 'We have a long way to go.'

After trudging down the steep, rock-strewn slope for more than an hour, the party arrived, weary and blackened, at a long ledge that led between a sharp cliff and a pond whose surface was entirely covered with a thick oil slick. As they watched, a great, heavy-winged water bird landed in the foul water with a soft plop and dissolved.

'Let us press on,' said Goodgulf. 'The pass cannot be far.'

With that he led the way around a stony ridge which jutted into the pond in front of them and obscured the rest of the mountain slope from view. The ledge grew narrower as it wound around the outcropping, and the company had to inch their way along. As they passed the bend, they saw in front of them the face of the mountain rising unbroken for hundreds of feet above them. Cut into the rocky wall was the entrance to some underground cavern, cunningly hidden by an enormous wooden door with huge wrought-iron hinges and a giant knob. The door was covered with a strange oath gracefully written in the Palmer runes of the dwarves, and so marvelously had it been constructed, that from a hundred feet away the tiny crack between wood and stone was completely invisible.

Arrowroot gasped. 'The Black Pit,' he cried.

'Yes,' said Gimlet, 'the fabled Nikon-zoom of my ancestor, Fergus Fewmet.'

'Dread Andrea Doria, curse of the living nipple,' said Legolam.

'But where is the pass?' asked Frito.

'The face of the land has changed since I was last abroad in this region,' said Goodgulf quickly, 'and we have been led, perhaps by Fate, a bit astray.'

ERGUS spake these words, and he said, This shall be my creed, whereby shall I live my life as it were a shining example of Virtue and Excellence, well worthy to be enshrined in Heaven as a model for all who are wise to follow. My creed shall into three parts, like Gaul, be divided. Firstly, I shall constrain myself to mind My Own Business. Secondly, I shall endeavour at all times and in all places to keep My Nose Clean by the most expedient possible means. Thirdly, and finally, I shall always exercise the utmost care to keep My Hands to Myself.

—PW1

'It would be wiser to seek again the pass, I judge,' said Arrowroot. 'It cannot be far.'

'Three hundred kilometers give or take a shilling,' said Goodgulf, a little sheepishly, and as he spoke, the narrow ledge which led back to the valley slid into the dark pond with a low grunt.

'That settles that,' said Bromosel testily. 'Yoo-hoo,' he cried, 'come and eat us,' and from far away a deep voice echoed, 'Me beastie, me do that thing.'

'It is a grim fate indeed that would lead us here,' said Arrowroot, 'or a gonzo Wizard.'

Goodgulf remained unperturbed. 'We must find the spell that opens this door, and soon. Already it grows dark.' With that he lifted his wand and cried:

Yuma palo alto napa erin go brae
Tegrin correga cremora olé.

The door remained in place, and Frito glanced nervously at the mass of oily bubbles that had begun to rise in the pond.

'If only I'd listened to my Uncle Poo-poo and gone into dentistry,' whined Pepsi.

'If I'd stayed at home, I'd be big in encyclopedias by now,' sniffled Moxie.

'And if I had ten pounds o' ciment and a couple o' sacks, you'd a' both gone for a stroll on that pond an hour ago,' said Spam.

Goodgulf sat dejectedly before the obstinate portal, mumbling spells.

'Pismo,' he intoned, striking the door with his wand. 'Bitumen. Lazlo. Clayton-Bulwer.' Save for a hollow thud, the door made no sign of opening.

'It looks grim,' said Arrowroot.

Suddenly the Wizard sprang to his feet. 'The knob,' he cried, and leading the pack sheep over to the base of the gate, stood on its back on tiptoe and turned the great knob with both hands. It turned easily, and with a loud squeaking the door swung open a crack.

Goodgulf quickly scrambled down, and Arrowroot and Bromosel tugged the door open a few more inches. At that moment, a great gurgling and belching arose from the center of the pond, and a large corduroy monster slowly lifted itself above the surface with a loud hiccup.

The company stood rooted to the ground in terror. The creature was about fifty feet tall, with wide lapels, long dangling participles, and a pronounced gazetteer.

'Aiyee!' shouted Legolam. 'A Thesaurus!'

'Maim!' roared the monster. 'Mutilate, mangle, crush. See HARM.'

'Quick,' cried Goodgulf. 'Into the cavern,' and the company hurriedly slipped one by one through the narrow crack. Last of all came Spam, who tried to squeeze the protesting sheep through the opening.

After two frenzied but unsuccessful attempts, he picked up the annoyed herbivore and threw him bodily into the beast's gaping mouth.

'Eatable,' said the giant creature between munches, 'edible, esculent, comestible. See FOOD.'

'I hope ye choke on it,' said Spam bitterly, as a clear image of a winged loin of lamb fluttered across his mind. He wiggled through the doorway and joined the rest of the company in the cavern. With a loud belch that shook the ground and filled the air with an aroma such as one meets concurrent with the rediscovery of a cheese that has long since gone to its reward, the beast slammed shut the door. The heavy boom reverberated into the depths of the mountain, and the little party found themselves in total darkness.

Goodgulf hastily withdrew a tinder box from his robes, and frantically striking sparks off the walls and floor, he managed to light the end of his wand, producing a flickering glow about half as bright as a dead firefly.

'Such magic,' said Bromosel.

The wizard peered ahead into the darkness, and perceiving that there was only one possible route, up a flight of stairs, he led the way into the deep gloom.

They traveled a considerable distance into the mountain along the passageway, which after the long flight of stairs leading up from the gate worked its way for the most part down, with countless changes of direction, until the air became quite hot and stuffy and the company very confused. There was still no source of light save for the flicker of Goodgulf's sputtering wand, and the only sound came from the sinister patter of following footsteps, the heavy breathing of North Koreans, the rattle of gumball machines, and the other hurly-burly of deep, dark places.

At length they came to a place where the passage divided into two, with both leading down, and Goodgulf signaled for a halt. Immediately there came a series of ominous gurgles and other-worldly tweets that suggested that the Four Horsemen of the Apocalypse were having a friendly rubber of bridge not a yard away.

'Let's split up,' said Bromosel.

'I've twisted my ankle,' said Pepsi.

'Whatever you do, don't make a sound,' said Arrowroot.

'Wa-zoo,' screamed Moxie, sneezing violently.

'Now here's my plan,' said Goodgulf.

'Bullets won't stop them,' said Bromosel.

'Whatever happens,' said Arrowroot, 'we must keep a close watch.'

The company, as a man, fell asleep.

When they awoke, all was quiet once more, and

after a hasty meal of cakes and ale, they addressed themselves to the problem of which passage to take. As they stood debating, there came from deep in the earth a steady drumbeat. *Dribble, dribble, dribble, shoot, swish.*

At the same time the air began to get hotter and thicker, and the ground started to tremble beneath their feet.

'There's no time to lose,' said Goodgulf, jumping to his feet. 'We must decide and quickly.'

'I say to the right,' said Arrowroot.

'Left,' said Bromosel.

Upon closer examination, the left way proved to be lacking a floor for some forty feet, and Goodgulf quickly set off down the other, with the rest of the company following close behind. The passage led precipitously down, and there were omens of an unappetizing nature along the way, including the whitening skeleton of a minotaur, the body of the Piltdown man, and a rabbit's battered pocket watch with the inscription 'To Whitey from the whole Wonderland crowd.'

Before long the passageway sloped more gently down until with a final plunge it led into a great chamber lined with huge metal lockers and dimly lit by a fiery glow. As they entered, the rumblings grew louder: *Dribble. Dribble. Fake. Dribble. Fake. Shoot.*

All at once a large body of narcs burst into the hall from the passage the company had followed and charged at them, waving hammers and sickles.

'Yalu, Yalu,' shouted their leader, brandishing a huge faggot.

'You dieth, G.I.,' cried the faggot.

'Stay here,' said Arrowroot. 'I'll scout ahead.'

'Keep me covered,' said Legolam, 'I'll head them off.'

'Guard the rear,' said Gimlet, 'I'll take the passage.'

'Hold the fort,' said Goodgulf, 'I'll circle around.'

'Stand fast,' said Bromosel, 'I'll draw them off.'

'Pyongyang panmunjom,' shouted the narc chieftain.

The company stampeded across the hall and out a side passage with narcs at their heels. As they rushed out, Goodgulf slammed shut the door in the narcs' faces and hastily put a spell on it.

'Hawley Smoot,' he said, striking the door with his wand, and with a smoky 'foof' the door disappeared, leaving the Wizard face-to-face with the puzzled narcs. Goodgulf quickly produced a lengthy confession, signed it, and thrusting it into the chieftain's hands, raced away up the passage to where the rest of the company stood at the far end of a narrow rope bridge which spanned a sharp chasm.

As Goodgulf stepped onto the bridge the passage

echoed with an ominous *dribble, dribble*, and a great crowd of narcs burst forth. In their midst was a towering dark shadow too terrible to describe. In its hand it held a huge black globe and on its chest was written in cruel runes, 'Villanova.'

'Aiyee,' shouted Legolam. 'A ballhog!'

Goodgulf turned to face the dread shadow, and as he did, it slowly circled toward the bridge, bouncing the grim sphere as it came. The Wizard reeled back and, clutching at the ropes, raised his wand. 'Back, vile hoopster,' he cried.

At this the ballhog strode forward onto the bridge, and stepping back, the wizard drew himself up to his full height and said, 'Avaunt, thin-clad one!'

Arrowroot waved Krona. 'He cannot hold the bridge,' he shouted and rushed forward.

'E pluribus unum,' cried Bromosel and leaped after him.

'Esso extra,' said Legolam, jumping behind him.

'Kaiser Frazer,' shouted Gimlet, running up to join them.

The ballhog sprang forward, and raising the dread globe over his head, uttered a triumphant cry.

'Dulce et decorum,' said Bromosel, hacking at the bridge.

'Above and beyond,' said Arrowroot, chopping a support.

'A far, far better thing,' said Legolam, slicing through the walkway.

'Nearer my God to thee,' hummed Gimlet, cutting the last stay with a quick ax stroke.

With a loud snap, the bridge collapsed, spilling Goodgulf and the ballhog into the abyss. Arrowroot turned away and, stifling a sob, ran along the passage with the rest of the company close behind. As they rounded a corner, they were dazzled by a sudden shaft of sunlight, and after dispatching a sleeping narc guard in a few short minutes, they scrambled out the gates and down the eastern stairs.

The stairs ran along a syrupy stream in which large gobs of multicolored goo were ominously bobbing. Legolam stopped and spat in it wistfully.

'It is the Spumoni,' he explained, 'beloved of the Elves. Do not drink of it – it causes cavities.'

The company hastened on into the shallow valley and in less than an hour stood on the west bank of the river Nesselrode, which the dwarves call Nazal-spray. Arrowroot signaled for a halt. The steps that had led down the mountain came to an abrupt end at the river's edge, and on either side of the narrow way the hills sloped off into wide, barren plains filled with wind gods, dolphins in sailor hats, and street directories.

'I fear that we have come to an uncharted region,'

said Arrowroot, peering under his hand into the distance. 'Alas, that Goodgulf is not here to guide us.'

'These are indeed tough bananas,' agreed Bromosel.

'Yonder lies Lornadoon, land of the Gone Elves,' said Legolam, pointing across the river to a scruffy-looking forest of dutch elms and knotty pines. 'Goodgulf would have surely led us there.'

Bromosel dipped a foot into the oozing river, and a fish stick and a side order of fried clams leaped into the air.

'Sorcery!' cried Gimlet as a tunaburger flew past his ear. 'Witchcraft! Deviltry! Isolationism! Free silver!'

'Aye,' said Legolam, 'the river is under a spell, for it is named after the fair elf-maid Nesselrode who had the hots for Menthol, God of After-Dinner Drinks. But the evil Oxydol, Goddess of Quick Tricks and Small Slams, appeared to her in the shape of a five-iron and told her that Menthol was two-timing with the Princess Phisohex, daughter of King Sano. At this Nesselrode became wroth and swore a great oath to kick Phisohex in the gut and get her mother, Cinerama, Goddess of Short-Term Loans, to turn Menthol into an erector set. But Menthol got wind of the plot and came to Nesselrode in the guise of a refrigerator, turned her into a river, and went west to sell encyclopedias. Even now, in the spring, the river softly cries, "Menthol, Menthol, you are one wazoo. One day I'm the elf next door and then *poof* I'm a river. You stink." And the wind answers, "Phooey." '

'A sad story,' said Frito. 'Is it true?'

'No,' said Legolam. 'There's a song, too,' and he began to sing:

> An elvin-maid there was of old,
>   A stenographer by day;
> Her hair was fake, her teeth were gold,
>   Her scent was that of cheap sachet.
>
> She thought that art was really 'keen,'
>   The top ten she could hum;
> Her eyes were full of Maybelline,
>   Her mouth, of chewing gum.
>
> Her head was full of men and clothes,
>   Her hair, of ratted curls;
> Her legs she wrapped in fine Sup-Hose,
>   For nights out with the girls.
>
> She met one morn an elvin-lad,
>   Who took her to the fights,
> And said he owned a spacious pad,
>   And went to law school nights.
>
> And so that night she gave her all
>   In back of his sedan;

So rich, she thought, so sharp and tall,
  A perfect family man.

But then he told her with a smirk,
  That he loved another,
And was a part-time postal clerk
  And lived home with his mother.

A silver tear rolled down her cheek
  As she bussed home by herself;
The same thing happened twice last week,
  (Oh, Heaven help the Working-elf!)

'It is best that we cross before nightfall,' said Arrowroot finally. 'There are tales of fungo bats and bloodsucking umpires in these parts.' Picking up his toilet kit, he waded into the soupy water, and the company followed behind. The water was nowhere more than a few feet deep, and the boggies had little difficulty making their way across.

'This is indeed a queer river,' said Bromosel, as the water lapped at his thighs.

On the far bank of the river they found a thick strand of dead trees covered with signs in Elveranto which said, COME TO FABULOUS ELF VILLAGE, VISIT THE SNAKE FARM, DON'T MISS SANTA'S WORKSHOP, and HELP KEEP OUR FOREST ENCHANTED!

'Lalornadoon, Lalornadoon,' sighed Legolam, 'wonder of Lower Middle Earth!'

At that, a door in the trunk of a large tree opened, revealing a small room filled with postcard racks, loudly clicking cuckoo clocks, and boxes of maple-sugar candies. A greasy-looking elf slipped out from behind a taffy machine.

'Welcome wagon,' he said, bowing low. 'I am Pentel.'

'Come hither, conastoga,' said Legolam.

'Well, well, well,' said the elf, coughing importantly, 'we are a bit out of season, aren't we?'

'We're just passing through,' said Arrowroot.

'No matter,' said Pentel. 'Plenty to see, plenty to see. On the left, your petrified tree, to the right your Echo Rock and your Natural Bridge, and just ahead your Old Wishing Well.'

'We've come from Doria,' Arrowroot continued. 'We're on our way to Fordor.'

The elf blanched. 'I hope you've enjoyed your visit to Lornadoon, Land of Magic,' he said quickly, and handing them a sheaf of folders and pack-horse stickers, he leaped into the tree and slammed and bolted the door.

'These are troubled times,' said Arrowroot.

Legolam opened one of the folders and pored over a map. 'It isn't far to the Elf Village,' he said finally, 'and unless the place has changed hands, Orlon's kin, Cellophane and the Lady Lavalier, still dwell there.'

'Elves,' grumbled Spam. 'Now I'm not saying Sorhed is right, but I'm not a-saying he's wrong, neither, if you get my drift.'

'Shut up,' said Legolam gravely.

After a hasty meal of frankincense and myrrh, the company set off down a wide path which Legolam identified on the map as Horror Lane, and from time to time mechanical dragons and goblins lurched unsteadily from rubber shrubs and yawned and grunted. But even the boggies remained unperturbed by these assaults, and in a few short hours the travelers arrived at the edge of a small grove of very petrified-looking trees from whose oddly symmetrical branches heavily corroded copper leaves dropped in unconvincing bunches.

As they stood wondering, the head of an elf-maid appeared at a bay window in the nearest tree and cried in the ancient tongue of the elves: '𝕲𝖗𝖊𝖊𝖙𝖎𝖓𝖌𝖋 𝖞𝖊 𝖔𝖑𝖉𝖊 𝖜𝖆𝖞𝖋𝖆𝖗𝖊𝖗𝖋.'

'Are there any more at home like you?' said Legolam, making the correct reply.

A moment later the door to the great tree swung open, and a short elf stepped out. 'Cellophane and Lavalier await you abovestairs,' he said, and led the company into the wide trunk. The tree was completely hollow, and the inside was covered with brick-design wallpaper. A circular staircase led through a hole in the ceiling to an upper story, and the elf motioned for them to ascend the narrow steps. As they reached the top, they found themselves in a room decorated much as the one below, but brightly lit by great wagon-wheel chandeliers which hung from the lofty roof. On a pair of tree stumps at the end of the room sat Cellophane and Lavalier, arrayed in rich muslin.

'Welcome to Lornadoon,' said Lavalier, rising slowly to her feet, and it seemed to the company that she was as fair as a young sapling or scrub oak. She had magnificent chestnut hair, and when she shook her head, handfuls of magnificent chestnuts dropped to the floor like rain. Frito toyed with the Ring and wondered at her great beauty. As he stood, as if in a trance, Lavalier turned to him and saw him toying with the Ring and wondering at her great beauty.

'I see, Frito,' she said, 'that as you toy with the Ring, you wonder at my great beauty.'

Frito gasped.

'Do not fear,' she said, solemnly tweaking his nose. 'Nasties we're not.'

Cellophane then rose and greeted each of the travelers in turn, and motioning for them to sit down on the rubber toadstools arranged around the room, bid them tell the tale of their adventures.

Arrowroot cleared his throat. 'Once upon a time,' he began.

'Call me Ishmael,' said Gimlet.

'Whanne in Aprille,' started Legolam.

'Hear me, oh Muse,' commenced Bromosel.

After some discussion, Frito told the whole story of the Ring, Dildo's party, the Black Schleppers, the Caucus of Orlon, Doria, and Goodgulf's untimely passing.

'Woodja, woodja, woo,' said Cellophane sadly when Frito had finished.

Lavalier sighed deeply. 'Your journey is long and hard,' she said.

'Yes,' said Cellophane, 'you bear a great burden.'

'Your enemies are powerful and merciless,' said Lavalier.

'You have much to fear,' said Cellophane.

'You leave at dawn,' said Lavalier.

After a hearty feast of cherubim and seraphim, Cellophane and Lavalier showed the weary travelers to rooms in a small tree nearby, and as Frito was preparing to enter, Lavalier drew him aside and brought him to a sheltered vale nearby, in the center of which stood a soiled birdbath in which a pair of sparrows were floating upside down.

'Poison,' explained Lavalier, flinging the feathered

corpora into the bushes. 'It's the only thing that even slows them down.' Thereupon she spat into the water, and a goldfish leaped into the air and cried, 'Give me your sevens.'

At that she leaned over the surface and whispered, 'Wilmot Proviso,' and the water began to boil, filling the air with a light odor of beef gumbo. Then it seemed to Frito that the surface became smooth, and there appeared the picture of a man squirting something into his nose.

'Commercials,' said Lavalier irritably.

In a moment the water cleared, and there came scenes of elves and dwarves dancing in the streets, wild revels in Minas Troney, happy debauches in the Sty, a large bronze statue of Sorhed being melted into tie clips, and finally Frito himself stirring on a pile of costume jewelry and smiling broadly.

'This bodes well,' declared Lavalier.

Frito rubbed his eyes and pinched himself. 'Then it is not all black?' he asked.

'The bath of Lavalier never lies,' said the Lady sternly, and leading Frito back to the rest of the company, disappeared in a heavy haze of Jungle Rape perfume.

Frito pinched himself one last time, then stumbled into the treehouse and fell into a deep sleep.

The surface of the basin remained black for a while,

then flickered and showed the triumphant reception of the S.S. *Titanic* in New York Harbor, the repayment of the French war debt, and the inaugural ball of Harold Stassen.

In the eastern sky, Velveeta, beloved morning star of the elves and handmaid of the dawn, rose and greeted Noxzema, bringer of the flannel tongue, and clanging on her golden garbage pail, bade him make ready the winged rickshaw of Novocaine, herald of the day. Thence came rosy-eyeballed Ovaltine, she of the fluffy mouth, and lightly kissed the land east of the Seas. In other words, it was morning.

The company rose, and after a hurried breakfast of yaws and goiters, Cellophane and Lavalier and their attendants led them through the wood to the banks of the great river Anacin where three small balsa rafts lay.

'It is the sad hour of parting,' said Lavalier solemnly. 'But I have for each of you a small gift to remind you of your stay in Lornadoon in the dark days to come.' So saying, she produced a large chest and drew out a handful of wondrous things.

'For Arrowroot,' she said, 'crown jewels,' and handed the surprised king a diamond-shaped pear and a plover's egg the size of an emerald.

'For Frito, a little magic,' and the boggie found in his hand a marvelous crystal globe filled with floating snowflakes.

She then gave each of the other members of the company something rich and strange: to Gimlet, a subscription to *Elf Life*, to Legolam, a Mah-Jongg set, to Moxie, a case of Cloverine Brand Salve, to Pepsi, a pair of salad forks, to Bromosel a Schwinn bicycle, and to Spam a can of insect repellent.

The gifts were quickly stowed away in the little boats along with certain other impedimenta needful for a quest, including ropes; tins of Dinty Moore beef stew; a lot of copra; magic cloaks that blended in with any background, either green grass, green trees, green rocks, or green sky; a copy of *Jane's Dragons and Basilisks of the World*; a box of dog yummies; and a case of Poland water.

'Farewell,' said Lavalier, as the company crammed themselves into the boats. 'A great journey begins with a single step. No man is an island.'

'The early bird gets the worm,' said Cellophane.

The rafts slipped out into the river, and Cellophane and Lavalier boarded a great boat-shaped swan and drifted a short distance beside them, and Lavalier sat in the prow and sang an ancient elvish lament to the heartbreaking timbre of steel drums:

Dago, Dago, Lassi Lima rintintin
Yanqui unicycle ramar rotoroot
Telstar aloha saarinen cloret
Stassen camaro impala desoto?
Gardol oleo telephon lumumba!
Chappaqua havatampa muriel
U canleada horsta wata, bwana,
Butyu canna makit drinque!

Comsat melba rubaiyat nirvana
Garcia y vega hiawatha aloo.
O mithra, mithra, I fain wud lie doon!
Valdaree valdera, que sera, sirrah,
Honi soit la vache qui rit.
Honi soit la vache qui rit.

('Oh, the leaves are falling, the flowers are wilting, and the rivers are all going Republican. O Ramar, Ramar, ride quickly on your golden unicycle and warn the nymphs and drag queens! Ah, who now shall gather lichee nuts and make hoopla under the topiaries? Who will trim my unicorns? See, even now the cows laugh, Alas, alas.' Chorus: 'We are the chorus, and we agree. We agree, we agree, we agree.')

As the tiny boats passed round a bend in the river, Frito looked back in time to see the Lady Lavalier gracefully sticking her finger down her throat in the ancient elvish farewell.

Bromosel looked ahead to where the meandering of the river had brought them face-to-face with the barely risen sun. 'The early bird gets hepatitis,' he grunted, and fell asleep.

Such was the enchantment of Lornadoon that although they had spent only a night in that magic land, it seemed like a week, and as they drifted down the river, Frito was filled with a vague fear that time was running out. He remembered Bromosel's ill-omened dream and noticed for the first time that there was a large blotch of lamb's blood on the warrior's forehead, a large chalk X on his back, and a black spot the size of a doubloon on his cheek. A huge and rather menacing vulture was sitting on his left shoulder, picking its teeth and singing an inane song about a grackle.

Not long after midday the river began to become narrow and shallow, and before long the way was completely blocked by an enormous beaver dam from which there emanated the grim slaps of beaver tails and the ominous whine of turbines.

'I had thought the way to the Isles of Langerhans was clear,' said Arrowroot. 'Now I see that the servants of Sorhed are at work even here. We can go no farther along the river.' The company paddled to the west bank, and drawing their boats onto the shore, ate a hurried meal of moon and sixpence.

'I fear these brutes may do us ill,' said Bromosel, pointing to the looming concrete mass of the dam.

As he spoke, a bulky figure waddled unsteadily across the stony shore. It was about four feet tall, very dark-complexioned, with a tail like a plank steak, a black beret, and wrap-around dark glasses.

'Your servant,' lisped the strange creature, bowing low.

Arrowroot eyed the brute thoughtfully. 'And who might you be?' he said at last, his hand falling to his sword hilt.

'An innocent traveler like yourselves,' said the brown figure, slapping his tail for emphasis. 'My horse threw a shoe or my boat sank. I don't remember which.'

Arrowroot sighed with relief. 'Well, you are welcome,' he said. 'I had feared you might be evil.'

The creature laughed indulgently, revealing a pair of front teeth the size of bathroom tiles. 'Hardly,' he said, munching absently on a piece of driftwood. Then with a great sneeze, his dark glasses fell to the ground.

Legolam gasped. 'A black beaver!' he cried, staggering back.

At that moment there came a great crashing in the nearby woods, and band of howling narcs and grunting beavers descended on the luckless party.

Arrowroot leaped to his feet. 'Evinrude,' he cried, and drawing the sword Krona, handed it hilt-first to the nearest narc.

'Joyvah Halvah,' shouted Gimlet, and dropped his adze.

'Unguentine,' said Legolam, putting his hands on his head.

'Ipso facto,' growled Bromosel, and unbuckled his sword belt.

Spam rushed over to Frito in the heat of the surrender and grasped him by the arm. 'Time to trot, bwana,' he said, drawing a shawl over his head, and the two boggies slipped down to the boats and out into the river before the charging narcs and their lumbering allies missed them.

The chief narc grabbed Arrowroot by the lapels and shook him fiercely. 'Where are boggies?' he screamed.

Arrowroot turned to where Frito and Spam had been standing and then to Moxie and Pepsi, who were hiding next to where Legolam and Gimlet were playing possum.

'You lie, you die,' said the narc, and Arrowroot couldn't help but notice the tone of malice which had crept into his voice.

He pointed to the boggies, and two narcs jumped forward and swept them up in the thighs they had by way of arms.

'There's been some mistake,' squealed Moxie. 'I haven't got it.'

'You've got the wrong man,' Pepsi shrieked. 'It's him,' he said, pointing to Moxie.

'That's the one,' cried Moxie, gesturing at Pepsi. 'I'd know him anywhere. Three-five, eighty-two, tattoo on left arm of rutting dragon, two counts of aiding and abetting known Ringbearer.'

The chief narc laughed cruelly. 'I give the rest of you ten to run,' he said, twirling a set of giant bolos with a threatening application of english. At that, Bromosel started to sprint, but catching his feet in his sword belt, he tripped and impaled himself on his pointed shoes.

'Ye doom is ycomme true,' he groaned. 'O, tell the Lacedomecians to man the torpedoes.' Then noisily shaking a large rattle, he expired.

The narc shook his head. 'Me, you don't need,' he said, and led the narc band away into the surrounding forest with Moxie and Pepsi.

Frito and Spam drifted silently across the river to the eastern bank, and drew their small boat onto the shore, while unseen in the shadow of the dam, a small gray figure on a green-and-yellow-spotted sea horse paddled warily along.

'Out of the bedpan, as the old Fatlip would say,' said

Spam, and fishing their overnight bags out of the craft, set out with Frito along the rising gorge that led to the next chapter.

VI

THE RIDERS
OF ROI-TAN

For three days, Arrowroot, Gimlet, and Legolam hunted the band of narcs, pausing in their relentless chase only for food, drink, sleep, a few hands of pinochle, and a couple of sightseeing detours. Tirelessly, the Ranger, dwarf, and elf pushed on after the captors of Moxie and Pepsi, often making a long march of up to three hundred yards before collapsing with apathy. Many times Stomper lost the scent, which was rather difficult since narcs are fond of collecting their droppings along the way into great, pungent mounds. These they carefully sculpted and molded into fearsome shapes as mute warning to any who might dare challenge their power.

But the narc mounds were growing fewer, indicating either that they had quickened their pace or had run out of roughage. In any case the trail grew fainter and the tall Ranger had to use his every skill to follow the barest traces of the company's passing, a worn ventilated shoe, a pair of loaded dice, and farther on, a pair of ventilated narcs.

The land was somber and flat, now populated only

by scrub brushes and other stunted growths. Occasionally they would pass a deserted village, empty save for a
stray dog or two, which bolstered the party's dwindling larder. Slowly they descended into the bleak Plain
of Roi-Tan, a hot, dry, and cheerless place.* To their
left were the dim peaks of the Mealey Mountains, and
to their right and far away the sluggish Effluvium. To
the south were the fabled lands of the Roi-Tanners,
sheepmen of no mean skill aboard a fighting bull
merino.

In earlier times the sheep-lords had been enemies of
Sorhed and had fought bravely against him at Brylopad
and Ipswitch. But now there were rumors of renegade
bands of mounted sheepmen who ravaged northern
Twodor, pillaging, raping, burning, killing, and raping.

Stomper halted in the march and let out a deep sigh
of dread and boredom. The narcs were leaving them
farther and farther behind. Carefully he unwrapped a
square of the elvish magic zwieback and broke it into
four equal pieces.

'Eat all, for this is the last we have,' he said, palming
the fourth piece for later.

Legolam and Gimlet chewed gravely and silently.
All around them they felt the malicious presence of
Serutan, the evil Wizard of Isinglass. His malignant

---

* Not unlike Passaic, New Jersey.

influence hung heavy in the air, his secret forces impeding their search. Forces that took many forms, but for the present came as the runs.

Gimlet, who, if possible, liked Legolam even less than at Riv'n'dell, gagged on his portion of zwieback.

'A curse on the elves and their punk grub,' he grumbled.

'And on the dwarves,' returned Legolam, 'whose taste is in their mouths.'

For the twentieth time the pair drew weapons, lusting for each other's chitlins, but Stomper intervened lest one be killed. The food was gone anyway.

'Hold and cease, halt, avaunt, put up thy swords, refrain from thy quarrel and stay thy hands,' he spake, raising a fringed glove.

'Buzz off, Hopalong,' growled the dwarf. 'I'll make casserole of that window dresser!'

But the Ranger drew his peacemaker and the fighting ended as quickly as it began, for even dwarves and elves do not relish a shiv in the back. Then, as the combatants sheathed their blades, Stomper's voice rang out again.

'Lo!' he cried, pointing to the south. 'Many riders approach like the wind!'

'Would that they rode *down*wind as well,' said Legolam, wrinkling his nose.

'Keen are the nostrils of the elves,' said Stomper.

'And light are their feet,' muttered the dwarf under his breath.

All three squinted at the dust on the distant horizon. That they were sheepmen there was no doubt, for the wind heralded their approach.

'Do you think they're friendly?' said Legolam, trembling like a leaf.

'That I cannot say,' said Stomper. 'If they are, we have no worries; if they are foes, we must escape their wrath through craft.'

'How?' asked Gimlet, seeing no hiding place on the flat plain. 'Do we fight or flee?'

'Neither,' said the Ranger, falling limp on the ground. 'We'll all play dead!'

Legolam and Gimlet looked at each other and shook their heads. There were few things on which they both agreed, but Stomper was definitely one of them.

'We may as well take a few with us,' said Gimlet, drawing his cleaver, 'for it's better to go with one's codpiece buttoned.'

The sheep-lords loomed larger and the fierce war-bleats of their mounts could now be heard. Tall and blond were the Roi-Tanners, wearers of helmets topped with cruel-looking spikes and small toothbrush mustaches. The wanderers saw too that they wore long boots and short leathern pants with suspenders and held long pikes that looked like lead-weighted dust-mops.

'They are savage of visage,' said Legolam.

'Aye,' said Stomper, peeking through his fingers. 'Proud and willful are the men of Roi-Tan, and they value highly land and power. But these lands are often those of their neighbors, and they are hence mickle unpopular. Though ignorant of letters, they are fond of song and dance and premeditated homicide. But warfare is not their only craft, for they run summer camps for their neighbors handsomely fitted out with the most modern oven and shower facilities.'

'Then these rascals cannot be all bad,' said Legolam hopefully. Just then they saw a hundred blades flash from a hundred sheaths.

'Bets?' said Gimlet.

As they watched helplessly, the line of riders bore down upon them. Suddenly the centermost figure, whose spiked helmet also boasted two longhorns, gave a vague hand signal to halt and the men reined to a stop in a display of astoundingly inept sheepmanship. Two of their fallen comrades were maimed in the milling, trampling confusion that followed.

As the screams and curses died down, the pronged leader cantered up to the three astride a bull merino of great stature and whiteness, its tail intricately braided with colored rubber bands.

'The jerk looks like a fork,' whispered Gimlet out of the corner of his thick-lipped mouth. The leader, shorter than the others by a head, looked at them suspiciously through twin monocles and brandished a battlemop. It was then that the company realized that the leader was a woman, a woman whose ample breastplate hinted at a figure of some heft.

'Vere ist you going and vat are you doing here when you are not to being here in der first place vhere you ist?' the leader demanded in rather garbled everybody-talk.

Stomper stepped forward and bowed low, falling on one knee and pulling his forelock. Then he kissed the ground at the sheep-lord's feet. He buffed her boots for good measure.

'Hail and greeting, O Lady,' lisped Stomper, the butter in his mouth freezing solid. 'We are wayfarers in your land searching for friends taken by the foul narcs of Sorhed and Serutan. Perhaps you have espied them. They are three feet tall with hairy feet and little tails, probably dressed in elvin cloaks and headed for Fordor to destroy Sorhed's threat to Lower Middle Earth.'

The captain of the sheepmen stared at the Ranger dumbly, then, turning to her own company, beckoned a rider.

'Medic! Hurry up, I haf vork for you. Und he ist der delirious, also!'

'Nay, beautiful Lady,' said Stomper, 'they of whom

I speak are boggies, or in the tongue of the elves, *hoipolloi*. I am their guide, who am called Stomper by some, though I have many names.'

'I bet you do,' agreed the leader, tossing her golden braids. 'Medic! Vhere *ist* you?'

Finally Arrowroot's explanations were accepted, and introductions were made all around.

'I ist Eorache, daughter of Eorlobe, Captain of der Rubbermark and Thane of Chowder. Dot means you ist nice to me or you ist not nothing to nobody no more,' said the ruddy-faced warrior. Suddenly her face darkened when she espied Gimlet, whom she studied suspiciously.

'Vat your name ist again?'

'Gimlet, son of Groin, Dwarf-Lord of Geritol and Royal Inspector of Meats,' said the stubby dwarf.

Eorache dismounted and inspected Gimlet at closer range, a tight frown on her lips.

'Dot's funny,' she said at last, 'you don't *look* dwarfish!' Then she turned to Stomper. 'Und *you*. Undershirt vas it?'

'*Arrow*shirt!' said Stomper. 'Arrowroot of Arrow-shirt!'

In a flash he had drawn gleaming Krona from its holster and flailed it about over his head as he cried, 'And this is Krona of he who has many names, he who is called Lumbago, the Lodestone, by the elves,

Dunderhead, heir to the throne of Twodor and true son of Arrowhead of Araplane, Conqueror of Dozens and seed of Barbisol, Top of the Heap and King of the Mountain.'

'Vell la-dee-dah,' said Eorache, eyeing the waiting medic. 'But I ist believing dot you ist not der schpies of der Serutan. He ist one schtinker, but he ist not der schtupiter also.'

'We have come from afar,' said Legolam, 'and were led by Goodgulf Grayteeth, Wizard to Kings and Fairy Godfather, second class.'

The sheepess raised her yellow brows and let both monocles fall from her watery blue eyes. 'Schhhhhh! Dot ist not der name to be dropping around here. Der King, mein vater, lost his favorite mount, Saniflush der Swift, to dot schyster und later finds dot der dice ist queerer than der three-legged troll! Then der poor scheep ist coming back a week later covered with fleas and forgetting dot she ist housetrained all over der King's new tapestry. Vhen der King catches him, der ist vun dead Vizard!'

'There is a sad wisdom in your words,' said Arrowroot, trying to snatch a peek down her halberd, 'for Goodgulf is no more. He met his fate o'er-matched in uneven contest with a ballhog in the Mines of Doria. The creature played not fairly with Goodgulf, mastering him with means foul and deceitful.'

'Der poetic justicer,' said Eorache, 'but I vill miss der old crank.'

'And now,' said Arrowroot, 'we are in quest of our two companions captured by narcs and born whither we know not.'

'Ach,' said the lady warrior, 've fixed der vagons of some narcs yesterday, but ve don't see any boggies. Vhat ve find ist some little bones in der stewpot, und I don't think they vas having spare ribs.'

The three companions observed ten seconds of silent farewell for their friends.

'Then how about a lift on your mutton-mushers?' said Gimlet.

'Hokay,' said Eorache, 'but ve ist going to Isinglass to fix too der vagon of dot schkunken Serutan.'

'Then you fight with us against him,' said Stomper. 'We had thought the sheep-lords to have thrown their lot with the evil Wizard.'

'Ve haf never vorked for dot creep,' said Eorache loudly, 'und even if ve *did* help him a little at first, ve were only following orders und it probably vasn't us dot you heard about because ve vas someplace else. Und anyvay, he vas vasting his time looking for some schtupider Ring vhat vasn't vorth nothing. Me, I don't believe in dot pixie-dust schtuff. Magic-schmagic, I saying.'

The rider clicked her heels together and made an

about-face, calling over her shoulder. 'So, you coming mit us or you staying here und maybe starving to death?'

Stomper fondled the last piece of magic zwieback in his pocket and weighed the alternatives, not over-looking the beefy charms of Eorache.

'Ve going mit you,' he said dreamily.

Pepsi was dreaming that he was a maraschino cherry atop a huge hot-fudge sundae. Shivering on a mountain of whipped cream he saw a monstrous mouth of sharpened fangs loom above him, drooling great gobbets of saliva. He tried to scream for help but his own mouth was full of hardened fudge sauce. The maw descended, breathing a hot, odorous wind . . . down, down it came . . .

'Wake up, youse jerks,' snarled a harsh voice. 'Th' boss want t' talk to ya! Har har har!' A heavy brogan kicked out at Pepsi's already bruised ribs. He opened his eyes to the night gloom and met the evil stare of a brutish narc. This time he screamed, but the gagged boggie only gurgled with fear, and as he struggled he remembered that he was still hog-tied like a prime roast.

Now it all came back to him, how he and Moxie had been taken prisoner by the band of narcs and forced to march south toward a destination that they dreaded, the Land of Fordor. But a hundred blond riders on fighting sheep had cut them off and now the narcs feverishly prepared for the attack they knew would come with the first rays of the sun.

Pepsi received another kick and then heard a second narc-voice speak to the first.

'Mukluk pushkin, boggie-grag babushka lefrak!' rasped the deeper voice, which Pepsi recognized as that of Goulash, the leader of Serutan's narcs, who accompanied the party of Sorhed's larger, more well-equipped henchmen.

'Gorboduc khosla!' snapped the larger narc, who returned his attention to the frightened boggies. Smiling fiendishly, he drew his curved grasswhip and laughed. 'Bet youse guys would give an arm an' a leg t' get outta here.' He raised his weapon above his neckless head with mock savagery and reveled in the boggies' cringing and protestation.

'I, Goulash, shall have th' pleasure of takin' youse groundhogs t' th' great Serutan hisself, master of the fighting Ohmahah, Nastiest of the Nasty and Bearer of the Sacred White Rock, soon t' be th' boss of alla Lower Middle Earth!'

Suddenly a hamfisted blow from behind sent the narc spinning like a lathe.

'I'll give *you* boss of alla Lower Middle Earth!' spat a louder, deeper voice.

Moxie and Pepsi looked up to see a gigantic bull narc, well over seven feet and four hundred pounds if a gram. Towering over the sprawled narc, the monster pointed arrogantly to the red nose emblazed on his own chest. It was Karsh of the fighting Otto-wah, leader of Sorhed's contingent, who had laid Goulash low.

'I'll boss of alla Lower Middle Earth *you*!' he reiterated. Goulash sprang to heavily shod feet and made an obscene gesture at Karsh.

'Slushfund tietack kierkegaard!' he screamed, stamping in anger before the larger narc.

'Ersatz!' bellowed Karsh as he angrily drew his four-foot snickersnee and deftly trimmed Goulash's fingernails to the elbow. The smaller narc scampered off to retrieve his arm, cursing a blue streak, which was already lapping at the ooze.

'Now,' said Karsh, turning back to the boggies, 'them bleaters is gonna jump us at dawn, so's I want the lowdown on this Magic Ring *right now*!' Reaching into a large leather bag, the narc withdrew an armful of shiny instruments and arrayed them on the ground in front of Pepsi and Moxie. There before them were a large bullship, a thumbscrew, a cat-o'-nine-tails, a rubber hose, two blackjacks, an assortment of surgical knives, and a portable hibachi with two red-glowing branding irons.

'I got ways t' make ya sing like canaries,' he

chuckled, stirring the hot coals with his long index finger. 'Youse each can have one from column A and two from column B. Har har har!'

'Har har har,' said Pepsi.

'Mercy!' yupped Moxie.

'Aw, come on, youse guys,' said Karsh, selecting an iron with the triple-bar 'S' of Sorhed, 'let me have a little fun before y' talk.'

'No, please!' said Moxie.

'Who wants it first?' laughed the cruel narc.

'Him!' chorused the boggies, indicating each other.

'Ho ho!' chortled the narc as he stood over Moxie like some housewife sizing up a kielbasa. He raised the flaming iron and Moxie screeched at the sound of a blow. But when he opened his eyes again, his torturer was still standing above him, looking oddly different in expression. It was then that the boggie noticed that his head was missing. The body collapsed like a punctured whoopee cushion, and over it, triumphant, was the leering figure of Goulash. He held a blade in his good hand of the type usually employed on troublesome hamhocks.

'Last taps! Gotcha last!' he cried, hopping from one foot to the other with glee. 'And now,' he hissed in the boggies' faces, 'my Master Serutan desires the whereabouts of th' Ring!' He drop-kicked Karsh's noggin a good twenty yards for emphasis.

'Ring, ring?' said Pepsi. 'You know anything about a ring, Moxie?'

'Not unless you mean my vaccination scar,' said Moxie.

'Come on, come on!' Goulash urged, slightly singeing the hair on Pepsi's right big toe.

'Okay, okay,' sobbed Pepsi. 'Untie me and I'll draw you a map.'

Goulash agreed to this in his greedy haste and loosened the bonds around Pepsi's arms and legs.

'Now bring the torch nearer so we can see,' said the boggie.

'Gnash lubdub!' exclaimed the excited narc in his own foul tongue as he clumsily juggled the blade and the torch in his one remaining hand.

'Here, better let me hold the sword for you,' offered Pepsi.

'Knish snark!' gibbered the fiend, waving the torch in anticipation.

'Now these are the Mealey Mountains, and this is the Effluvium,' said Pepsi, scratching the ground with the sharp point of the shiny blade.

'Krishna rimsky-korsikov!'

'. . . and this is the Great Turnpath . . .'

'Grackle borgward!'

'. . . *and this is your gall bladder, right above your chitlins!*'

'Gork!' objected the narc as he fell to earth, opened from end to end like a pillow case. As his internal organs noisily shut down, Pepsi freed Moxie and they began threading their way through the narc battle lines, hoping not to be seen as the warriors prepared for the battle that would surely come with the first rays of the sun. Tiptoeing around a party of narcs busily honing their cruel knives, the boggies heard the low, gurgling song that they half sung, half belched in time with a spastic rhythm provided by one who repeatedly bashed his head against his iron helmet. The words were strange and harsh to their ears as they passed by in the dark:

> From the Halls of Khezaduma
> To the shores of Lithui
> We will fight King Sorhed's battles
> With tooth and nail and knee . . .

'Shhh,' whispered Pepsi as they crawled over open ground, 'don't make any noise.'

'Okay,' whispered Moxie.

'What's all that whisperin'?' growled a voice in the dark, and Pepsi felt a long-nailed hand grab at his lapel. Without thinking, Pepsi lashed out with his toenails and ran past, leaving the guard writhing on the ground holding the one area neither protected by his armor nor by his group insurance policy.

The boggies took off like a shot past the surprised narcs.

'The forest! The forest!' cried Pepsi, just ducking an arrow that neatly parted his hair to the bone. Shouts and confused alarums rang out on every side as they ran to the safety of the wood, for as luck would have it, the fierce *blaat* of the Roi-Tanners' war horns sounded the beginning of their attack. Diving for cover, the boggies watched with frightened eyes as the bloodthirsty sheep-lords advanced on the narcs, a hundred war-bleats echoing as one in the dawn light. The escaped prisoners forgotten, the narcs stood their ground as wave upon wave of woolly death crashed down upon them, battlemops thudding with a dreadful report against foot-thick skulls. Distant screams and blows reached the boggies' ears and they watched open-mouthed the carnage that followed. The outnumbered narcs gave way, and the slavering merinos charged this way and that, butting and kicking, fighting as mean and as dirty as their berserk riders. A handful of narcs could be seen with their cleavers thrown down and waving a white flag. The victors smiled broadly, surrounded them, and began hacking and hewing, tossing heads about like soccer balls. Laughing like loons, the merry band mirthfully relieved the corpses of their wallets and fillings. Pepsi and Moxie averted their faces from the slaughter, fighting their nausea unsuccessfully.

'Ho ho ho! The sheepers do not play at their craft.'

Moxie and Pepsi looked up with a start toward the green trees. They knew that they had heard a low, rumbling voice, but they saw no one.

'Hulloo?' they said uncertainly.

'Not "hulloo," *ho ho ho!*' returned the voice.

The brothers searched the woods for the source of the laugh, but not until a huge, green eye winked did they see the huge giant standing against the tall forest right in front of them. Their jaws dropped at the sight of an immense figure, fully eleven feet tall, standing before them with his hands coyly at his sides. He was bright green from head to foot (size fifty-six, triple-Z). A broad, pastel-green smile broke upon its face, and the monster laughed again. As the boggies retrieved their jaws, they noticed that the giant was naked save for a parsley G-string and a few cabbage leaves in his feather-cut locks. In each great hand was a package of frozen stringbeans, and across his chest a green banner proclaimed, TODAY'S SPECIAL, FIVE CENTS OFF ALL CREAMED CORN.

'No, no,' moaned Pepsi, 'it . . . it *couldn't* be!'

'Ho ho ho, but it is,' guffawed the immense figure, half man, half broccoli. 'I am called Birdseye, Lord of the Vee-Ates, oft called the jol—'

'Don't say it!' cried Moxie, holding his furry ears with horror.

'Be not afraid,' grinned the affable vegetable. 'I want to make *peas* with you.'

'No, no!' moaned Pepsi, nibbling his tie clip in frenzy.

'Come come,' said the giant, '*lettuce* go and meet my subjects who live in the forest. They cannot be *beet*. Ho ho ho!' The green apparition doubled over at his own *bon mot*.

'Please, please,' pleaded Pepsi, 'we can't take it. Not after all we've been through.'

'I must insist, my friends,' said the giant, 'the people of my realm are off to war on the evil Serutan, eater of cellulose and friend of the black weeds who every day strangle us more and more. We know you to be his enemy too, and you must come with us, and help defeat the cabbage-murderer.'

'Well, all right,' sighed Pepsi, 'if we gotta—'

'—we gotta,' sighed Moxie.

'Sigh not,' reassured the giant, as he slung the two boggies over his kelly green shoulder blades, 'being Lord of the Vee-Ates is not easy either, particularly on my *celery*. Ho!'

The boggies kicked and screamed, attempting a final escape from the towering bore.

'Struggle not,' he said soothingly, 'I know a couple of *peaches* that will be just right for you meat-things. You will love them, they are—'

'—quite a *pear*,' muttered Pepsi.

'Hey,' burbled the giant, 'that is a *good* one. Wish I had said that!'

'You will,' sobbed Moxie, 'you will.'

Arrowroot, Legolam, and Gimlet massaged their aching muscles under a shaded coppice as the Roi-Tanners watered their slobbering mounts and looked over the weaker of them for the evening meal. Three long days had they ridden hither and thither over rocky ground and smooth toward the dreaded fortress of Serutan the Gauche, and relations among the company had deteriorated somewhat. Legolam and Gimlet never tired of baiting each other, and when the elf laughed at the dwarf as he fell from his mount and was dragged raw the first day out, Gimlet retaliated by slipping Legolam's steed a strong laxative on the sly. The second day thus found the elf being borne in panicky circles and zigzags by his ailing mount and that night he revenged himself by shortening the right rear leg of Gimlet's merino, causing its rider many long hours of violent seasickness on the following day's ride. It had not been a tranquil journey.

In addition, it appeared to both Gimlet and Legolam that something odd had come over Arrowroot since they had met the Roi-Tanners, for he sat listlessly in the saddle and crooned to himself, always glancing covertly toward the leader of the sheep-lords, who spurned his advances. The last night of the ride Legolam awoke to find the Ranger absent from his pup tent and a huge commotion in the bushes nearby. Before the elf could remove his hairnet and buckle on his weapon, Arrowroot returned more melancholy than ever, nursing a sprained wrist and two heavily purpled eyes.

'Ran into a tree,' was his only explanation.

But Isinglass and the fortress of Serutan were now near, and the hard riding could be put by for an evening of rest.

'Ook!' yelped Gimlet painfully as he hunkered down upon a mossy knoll, 'that damned four-legged pot roast busted my coccyx for sure.'

'Then ride on your head,' said Legolam in a snide tone of voice, 'it is much the softer and less valuable.'

'Fetch off, hairdresser.'

'Toad.'

'Poop.'

'Creep.'

Jingling spurs and the thwapping of a riding crop interrupted the discussion. The three companions watched as Eorache trundled her bulk up the knoll to meet them. She slapped the dust and lanolin from her metal studded jackboots and shook her horns dubiously.

'You two schtill machen mit der nasty names?' She contemptuously avoided the round, ardent eyes of

Arrowroot and laughed aloud. 'In der vaterland ve haf no argumenters,' she reprimanded, drawing several dirks for emphasis.

'The lads are but weary after their long ride,' cloyed the smitten Ranger, nibbling her heels playfully, 'but eager to do battle, as I am to prove my worthiness in your azure eyes.'

Eorache gagged audibly and spat a large, brown quid against the wind. She stomped away in disgust.

'Wrong number,' said Gimlet.

'Worry not,' sympathized Legolam, throwing a more-than-companionable arm around Arrowroot, 'them dames are all alike, poison, every last one of them.'

Arrowroot broke free, sobbing inconsolably.

'Der goes vun sick booby,' said the dwarf, pointing to his head.

Darkness was falling and the campfires of the Roi-Tanners began flickering. Over the next hill lay the valley of Isinglass, now renamed Serutanland by the scheming Wizard. Dejected, the Ranger shuffled among the resting warriors, hardly hearing their proud song, roared above the clinking of foamy steins:

> Ve ist der merry, gay Roi-Tanners,
> Who like der boots, salutes und banners.
> Ve ride der scheeps in vind and vheather
> Mit vhips und spurs und drawers of leather.

> *Ve dance und sing und valse und two-step*
> *Und never ever mach der goose-step.*
> *Peace iss vhat ve vant und do have,*
> *Und a piece of anything you have.*

Men frolicked about the fires, laughing and joking. Two blood-slathered contestants hacked at each other with sabers to the gloating cheers of flaxen-haired spectators, and farther on a gathering of warriors bellowed with mirth as they did something unattractive to a dog.

But the scene cheered him not. Heartsick, he walked on into the darkness, saying, 'Eorache, my Eorache,' softly over and over to himself. Tomorrow he would display such acts of valor that she would have to pay attention to him. He leaned against the tree and sighed.

'Really got it, huh?'

Stomper jumped back with a cry, but it was the familiar pointed head of Gimlet that poked through the leaves.

'I did not see thee approach,' said Arrowroot, sheathing his sword.

'Just trying to lose that jerk,' said the dwarf.

'Who's a jerk, sirrah?' snapped Legolam, who had been molesting a chipmunk behind the tree.

'Speak o' the devil,' groaned Gimlet.

The three sat under the broad branches and thought

upon the hard travels they had made, seemingly to no purpose. What good would the defeat of Serutan be if Sorhed claimed Frito's Ring for his own? Who could resist his power then? For a long while they brooded.

'Isn't it about time for a *deus ex machina*?' said Legolam wearily.

Suddenly there was a loud *pop* and a bright burst of light that momentarily blinded the shocked three. The acrid odor of cheap flash-powder filled the air, and the companions heard a distinct *thump* followed by a louder *oof*! Then through the swirling confetti, they saw a shining figure dressed all in white, brushing the twigs and dirt from his spotless bell-bottoms and gleaming a-go-go boots. Above the white Nehru jacket and cheesy medallion was a neatly trimmed gray beard set off by oversized wraparound shades. The whole ensemble was topped off by a large white panama with a matching ostrich plume.

'Serutan!' gasped Arrowroot.

'Close, but no cigar,' cackled the brilliant figure as he flicked a bit of invisible dust from his tailored shoulder. 'Pray try again. It is a sad thing indeed when old pals are recognized not!'

'Goodgulf?!' cried the three.

'None other,' said the aged fop. 'You seemed astonished that I have reappeared.'

'But how did – did you . . . ?' began Legolam.

'We thought the ballhog . . .' said Gimlet.

The old wizard winked and straightened his vulgar medallion.

'My story is a long one indeed, and I am not the same Goodgulf Grayteeth that you once knew. I have undergone many changes, no thanks to you, I might add.'

'Yah, a little Clairol on the temples and a trim,' whispered the observant dwarf.

'I heard that!' said Goodgulf, scratching a razor-cut sideburn. 'Take not too lightly my present form, for my powers are even mightier.'

'But how did you—'

'Much have I journeyed since we last met, and much have I seen, and there is much I would tell thee,' said Goodgulf.

'Anything but the name of your tailor,' said Gimlet. 'Where'd you get those duds, anyway? I thought Halloween was months off yet.'

'A most delightful little boutique in Lornadoon. It's me, don't you think?'

'More than you know,' agreed the dwarf.

'But how did—' began Legolam again.

The Wizard made a sign for silence.

'Know now that I am no longer the Wizard of old. My spirit has been purged, my nature has been altered, my image has been remade. There is little of the former self that in me remains.' With a flourish, Goodgulf doffed his panama in a low bow. 'I am completely transformed.'

'Bets?' grunted Gimlet as he saw five aces fall out of the hat.

'But Goodgulf!' exclaimed the elf impatiently. 'You have not yet told us how you survived the clutches of the ballhog, lived through the flames, recovered from the fall into the boiling pit, and escaped the blood-thirsty narcs to find us here!'

As the stars grew brighter in the velvet sky over-head, the elf, dwarf, and Ranger gathered around the radiant sage to hear the tale of his miraculous, impossible salvation.

'Well,' began Goodgulf, 'once out of the pit . . .'

VII

SERUTAN SPELLED
BACKWARDS IS MUD

The plaintive twitterings of morning birds woke Legolam, who stared sleepily into the rising sun. Looking
about, he saw all the company asleep save Goodgulf,
who idly played solitaire on sleeping Gimlet's hump.

'You cannot put a knave on a king. That's cheating,'
cautioned the elf.

'But I can put my fist down your gullet,' countered
the witty old conjurer, 'so why do not thee make a
cuckoo clock or whatever you do with your spare time.
I am meditating.'

But the elf looked at the Wizard with fondness. Half
the night they had sat up and listened to Goodgulf's
tales of strange wanderings and brave deeds. Tales full
of Goodgulf's courage and cunning against unnameable
enemies. Tales obvious to all as a pack of preposterous
lies. If Goodgulf had been transformed, he had not
been transformed much. What is more, Gimlet's watch
was missing.

Slowly the rest of the party roused themselves,
Arrowroot last, partially because of his befuddled
mooning over the fair Roi-Tanner, and partially

because he couldn't fasten his drop-seat underwear. Carefully the Ranger prepared the company's austere breakfast of eggs, waffles, bacon, grapefruit, pancakes, hot oatmeal, fresh-squeezed orange juice, and golden cheese blintzes. No one, the company agreed early in the quest, could make blintzes like old Arrowroot.

'Zo, you ist up, finally,' growled a voice. All heads turned to Eorache, tricked out in her best boots, spurs, and armor. Through her nose was thrust a fierce-looking chicken bone.

'Ah, dressed to kill,' chuckled Goodgulf as he rose to greet the surprised captain.

'*You!*' gasped Eorache.

'You were expecting maybe Beowulf?'

'But – but ve thought dot you vere kaput mit der ballhog,' said the Roi-Tanner.

'It is a long tale,' said Goodgulf, taking a deep breath.

'Then save it,' interrupted Eorache. 'Ve have der fighting to do mit der Serutanner. Coming mit me, please.'

The company followed Eorache to the rest of the warriors, all mounted on their fiery, champing steeds, eager as their riders for battle. Cheerfully they greeted their leader with a clenched fist of salute and whispered amused comments about the odd Ranger that followed her around like a demented basset.

The party mounted. Eorache grudgingly gave Thermofax, the fastest of all the Roi-Tanner's sheep, to Goodgulf. Then, as the Riders burst into song, they rode west toward Isinglass.

They had not ridden but two hours before they reached a crested hill and Eorache bellowed the order to halt. Down in the low valley lay the pastel pink-and-blue walls of Serutan's mighty fortress. The entire city was ringed with walls, and around the walls was a pale-lavender moat crossed by a bright-green drawbridge. Pennants flapped in the breeze bravely and the tall towers seemed verily to goose the clouds.

Beyond the walls the expedition saw the many wonders that had lured countless tourists through its portals in the past. Amusements of all descriptions lay within: carnivals and side-shows under permanent tents, fairies' wheels and gollum-coasters, tunnels of troth, griffin-go-rounds and gaming houses where a yokel could lose an idle hour, and if he wasn't careful, his jerkin. Years before, when Serutan still showed a fair face to the world, Goodgulf had worked in such a house as a croupier for 'Ye Wheel of Ye Fortune.' But only for a short time. Why he left and why he had been forever barred from Serutanland, as the evil Wizard renamed it, no one knew. And Goodgulf wasn't telling.

The company stared with apprehension at the

motionless wheels and tarpaulined exhibits. At the looming battlements stood rows of archers and pike-men, behind them caldrons of boiling farina. Above the ramparts rose a huge sign with the face of a cartoon character made famous through comic scrolls and innumerable shoddy toys. It was the visage of Dickey Dragon that simpered at the riders above the letters that read WELCOME TO SERUTANLAND. ALL RIDES TUPPENCE ON SUNDAYS. Everywhere, they noticed, were the brainless grins of Dickey Dragon. Pennants, signs, walls all bore that same idiotic, tongue-lolling face. But now that once-beloved creature had revealed itself to be the symbol of its creator's lust for power, a power that had to be ended.

'A mighty fortress is our Dickey Dragon,' said Goodgulf, ignoring the groans of those around him.

'Ja,' agreed Eorache, 'der Serutanner macht der mint mit der Dickey Dragon hats und der Dickey Dragon sweatshirts und der Dickey Dragon dis und der Dickey Dragon dot. One rich schtinker, der Serutanner ist.'

Goodgulf agreed that this was so, and that when they had been friends he had not been a bad sort.

'But this was all a sham and a front for his real purposes,' he added, 'and for that we must conquer him.'

'But how?' asked Legolam.

'Der diversionary tactic!' exclaimed Eorache, her chicken bone quivering. 'Ve need some dumkopf to draw dere attention vhile ve attack from der rear.' She paused and looked slyly at the love-struck Ranger out of the corner of her eye. 'Dot dumb – er, *hero* vould melt der heart of any fraulein, I thinking.'

Stomper's ears perked up like a randy boxer and he drew his blade, crying, 'Krona! I will undertake this mission for thy glory and honor, that I may win from you admiration, though I not return.' Clumsily, he goaded his truculent merino to her side and kissed a calloused hand. 'But first, I ask a token from thee, fair Eorache, that my valor may attempt to equal thy matchless charms. A token I ask of thee.'

Puzzled for a second, Eorache nodded her horned head and unbuckled her thick leather wrist-strengthener and handed the metal-studded strap to Arrowroot who fastened it joyfully around his neck.

'Hokay dere ist der token,' she said, 'now *raus!*'

Without another word he galloped down the slope toward the drawbridge amid the cheers of the war party. Faster and faster he sped as the rest circled under the cover of the ridge. Then, just as the merino's sharp hooves approached the portal into the fortress, the bridge was quickly raised up, revealing a familiar scaly grin painted on the underside, along with the legend, SORRY FOLKS. CLOSED FOR THE SEASON. But

Stomper's momentum carried him irresistibly onward until he plunged headlong into the lavender moat. Thrashing in the water, Stomper yelled with fear, for the moat became alive with sharp, rasping beaks. Great snapping turtles massed upon the drowning Ranger, and archers, noticing the commotion for the first time, began peppering the crackpot with crack pot-shots.

Eorache, hearing his cries, rode over the crest and saw Stomper floundering in the moat, assailed on all sides. Barking a Roi-Tanner oath, she raced down to the moat and sprang from her mount after him, locking his head in the crook of her muscular arm, and made for the shore. Then, as the party watched with awe, she stood up in the two-foot depths and scampered to safety, two water-and-arrow-logged merinos at her heels.

A great cheer rose from the Roi-Tanners as their leader trotted smartly back to the hill, the gasping Ranger still in tow. Muttering under her breath, she applied artificial respiration to Stomper, who choked up a surprising quantity of the moat and several small turtles. The vicious reptiles had torn away much of his raiment, leaving only his undergarments, which the lady noticed had the Royal Crown of Twodor embroidered on the backflap.

'Hey!' she exclaimed to the semiconscious Ranger.

'You got der Royal Crown of der Twodor embroidered on der backflap.'

'Aye,' said Goodgulf, 'for he is the true King of these and all lands of Twodor.'

'No kidding?' said Eorache, her eyes widening with concupiscence. 'Hmmm. Maybe der dumkopf ist hokay after all.' To the surprise of all, she began to murmur softly to Stomper as she threw him over her shoulder and gently burped him.

'There is no time for courtly pastimes,' said Goodgulf. 'Our diversion has failed and the enemy is now forewarned of our intentions. The hour to strike has passed and we are lost.'

'Does that mean we can go home now?' asked Legolam.

'No!' said the Wizard, his medallion flashing in the sun, 'for I see in the distance a vast army marching.'

'Nuts,' said Gimlet. 'I thought we could call it a day.'

With fearful eyes they all watched as a dark mass spread over a distant hill and moved toward them with alarming speed. Whether friend or foe, no one could discern. For many minutes they watched until cornets sounded from the battlements of Serutanland.

'They must be narc reinforcements come to destroy us all!' wailed the elf. 'Sorhed has sent a great army against us!'

'No!' cried the Ranger. 'They are not narcs, they are not like anything that I have seen.'

The others saw that this was true. Rank upon rank of huge, warlike vegetables were massing toward Serutanland, led by a monumental creature. An eldritch song thundered:

> All hail Vee-Ates, gather round!
> With greens held high and roots in ground!
> Cabbage, Eggplant, Cuke, and Carrot
> Purée narcs with club and garrot!
>
> Squash their pulp up into bits
> Slash their rinds and spit out the pits!
> Make their juice spout like a geyser
> And grind them all to fertilizer!

'Ho ho ho!' rang through the land and the frightened sheep milled in confusion like sheep. Dumbstruck, the party saw squads of squash, platoons of potatoes, companies of kumquats, battalions of beets, and regiments of radishes, all tramping to a martial air played by a fifty-piece rutabaga marching band. Beyond the endless rows were even more formations; determined-looking avocados, stalwart scallions and brawny eggplants.

The very ground shook at the rhythmic rootsteps of the horde, the air crackled with their thousand chattering, piping warcries.

Proudly, at the head of the column strode the green general, who had added a pair of cornsilk epaulets to his meager attire. On each shoulder was a familiar figure in addition, and Goodgulf was the first to see.

'It's the two runts, by cracky!' he cried.

And it was true. Moxie and Pepsi sat unsteadily on Birdseye's shoulders, both waving frantically at Goodgulf and the rest.

The acres of produce tramped directly to the walls of Serutanland and arranged themselves in battle formation. Through a glass lent by Eorache, Arrowroot saw consternated narcs first gaping, then rushing about the ramparts in panic.

'Ho ho ho!' thundered the giant. 'Be it known, Serutan, that the Vee-Ates are before you. Surrender or be pulped!'

At first there was no response from the fortress. Then a great voice replied to the giant with an earth-shaking raspberry.

'I take it then,' said the giant, 'that you wish to fight.' Without another word the giant strode back to his lines and began barking orders to his followers, who quickly obeyed, running hither and thither to set up formations and engines of war.

Great watermelons half walked, half rolled to the edge of the moat, followed by enormous potatoes who leapt heavily upon the melons, firing a deadly hail of seeds to rake the ramparts clean of narcs. The narcs fell like fruit flies while the onlookers from the hill applauded wildly.

Then a column of sweet potatoes forded the moat, ignoring the arrows that sunk deep into their pulp. Half submerged in the turtle-infested waters, the potatoes sprouted long, winding tendrils that climbed the sheer face of the walls, entwining around any protrusion. The vines served as scaling ladders for the hordes of commando cucumbers that hastily clambered up to challenge the defenders. Simultaneously the giant brought out a huge, wheeled catapult and aligned it toward the wall.

'Der gas varfare!' shouted Eorache, guessing his plan.

The puzzled watchers soon learned what the Roi-Tanner had meant, for fully three companies of suicide scallions appeared and began piling into the great scoop of the catapult. When the trip was released, the eight-foot onions soared in a high arc over the walls and set up a huge cloud of acrid fog upon impact. Through the glass the party saw the narcs feverishly wiping their streaming eyes with dirty black hand-kerchiefs. Ballistas of kamikaze kumquats rained death down upon the barricades, and deafening reports of aerial popcorns toppled parapets on the heads of Serutan's henchmen.

But the narcs still fought back desperately, their long blades flashing, dripping with vitamin-packed gore. The ramparts were littered with chopped parsley, diced onion, and grated carrots. Rivers of red tomato juice ran over the stones, and a ghastly salad floated in the moat.

Seeing that the fighting on the walls was yet undecided, the tall green commander ordered up another weapon, a pumpkin the size of a Mack truck. Nodding to his commands, the weighty squash rumbled over the moat on the backs of his slain comrades. Peppered with arrows, the great orange warrior stood before the raised drawbridge and immediately began butting it with its tremendous bulk. The whole wall shook and trembled. Again and again he crashed against the door while frantic defenders poured vats of steaming oatmeal down on the attacker. Parboiled yet undaunted, the brave pumpkin stepped back several yards and got one final running start, then rushed at the door full tilt. There was a titanic crash and the door seemed to explode into shards and splinters. The dazed battering-squash reeled back dizzily, staggered, shrugged its broad round shoulders, and split in half. Seeds ran out and mingled with the still-warm squeezings of brother warriors. For a moment all fell silent. Then, with a great cry, all the Vee-Ates rushed across the sundered shell and raged into the city. After them charged the Roi-Tanners and the company, eager to avenge its valorous end.

The final engagements inside the walls were short and bloody. Gimlet sang lustily as he swung at the wounded narcs and dismembered their inert defenseless corpses. Arrowroot and Legolam valiantly disposed of a number of brawny foes from behind and Goodgulf offered hearty exhortations and sound advice from the safety of a crumbled parapet. But it was the Roi-Tanner maiden and her cronies who took the day's honors as they destroyed the remaining narcs. Arrowroot sought out Eorache through the melee and found her gleefully mincing a narc fully half her size and singing an old Roi-Tanner drinking song. She saw him wave timidly at her. She smiled, winked, and tossed him a round object.

'Hey! King! Catch!'

Clumsily the Ranger fielded the souvenir. It was the head of a narc. Its final expression was one of extreme annoyance.

At last the fighting was over and the long-parted friends ran to each other with joyful greetings.

'Joyful greetings!' cried Moxie and Pepsi.

'The same and more to you, I'm sure,' said Goodgulf, stifling a yawn of recognition.

'Hail fellow well met,' bowed Legolam, 'may your dandruff worries be over forever.'

Gimlet limped over to the two boggies and forced a smile.

'Pox vobiscum. May you eat three balanced meals a day and have healthful, regular bowel movements.'

'How comes it,' said Arrowroot, 'that we meet in this strange land?'

'It is a tale long in the telling,' said Pepsi, pulling out a sheaf of notes.

'Then save it,' said Goodgulf. 'Have thee seen or heard news of Frito and the Ring?'

'Nary a peep,' said Moxie.

'Same here,' said Gimlet. 'Let's eat.'

'No,' said the Wizard, 'for we have not yet found the evil Serutan.'

'Nertz,' said Gimlet. 'It's already past lunch.'

Together with Birdseye and Eorache, the company sought out the evil magician. Word spread that Serutan and his loathsome companion Wormcast had been seen in Isintower, the tallest parapet in Serutanland, famous for the rotating restaurant high atop the shaft.

'He's up there,' a celery said. 'He jammed the elevators, but he's treed just the same.'

'Ho ho ho,' observed the giant.

'Shut up,' added Goodgulf.

High above them they saw the round, turning

restaurant with its flashing sign that read SERUTAN'S
TOP O' THE MARK. Under it a glass door swung open. A
figure appeared at the railing edge.

'Dot's him!' cried Eorache.

In face he looked much like Goodgulf, but his
raiment was strange to see. The Wizard was dressed
in a full-length leotard of fire-engine red and a long
cape of black sateen. On his head were pasted black
horns and at his buttocks was attached a barbed tail. He
held an aluminum pitchfork and wore cloven patent-
leather loafers. He laughed at the company below.

'Ha ha ha ha ha.'

'Come thee then down,' called Arrowroot, 'and
what to thee is coming, taketh. Open thy door and let
us in.'

'Nay,' cackled Serutan, 'not by the hair of my
chinny-chin-chin. Let us instead work this out like
sane, reasonable people.'

'Vork-schmork,' screamed Eorache. 'Ve vant your
miserable schkin!'

The evil wizard drew back in mock fear, then
returned to the edge and smiled. His voice was
soothing and melodious, dripping with sweet intona-
tions like a melting Fudgsicle. The company stood in
awe of his Sucaryled words.

'Let's backtrack,' continued Serutan. 'Here I am
with my little concern making an honest farthing by the

sweat of my brow. Suddenly a merger of competitors crash right through my corporate holdings trying to drive me out of the market. You have taken my liquid assets and nullified my small merchandizing staff. It's a clear-cut case of unfair business practices.'

'Hey,' said the giant to Goodgulf, 'that guy's got a good *head* on his shoulders. No wonder he reaps so much *cabbage*.'

'Shut up,' Goodgulf agreed.

'Now I have a proposition,' said Serutan, gesturing with the point of his tail, 'and though I'm not married to this idea, I thought I'd run it up the parapet and see if anybody pulls his forelock. Now I'll concede that I wanted a piece of the action, but it's that evil Sorhed who wants the whole ball of wax. As I see it, we form a new organization wherein I'll sign over a controlling interest in Dickey Dragon and its subsidiaries for my old executive position and yearly stock options on any old Rings we may come across along the way. Throw in thirty percent of the booty we get in Fordor and I'll let you have my partner Wormcast for free. He's responsible for this little proxy fight anyway.'

An anguished scream came from inside the tower and a bowl of wax fruit just missed Serutan's skull. A scrawny old man in a messenger boy's uniform appeared for a second and shook his fist.

'Garrrsch!' he sputtered.

Serutan picked up the protesting Wormcast and casually tossed him over the railing.

'Aaaaaaaaaarrrrrrrrrrrrrggggggghhhh!' said Wormcast.

The evil henchman hit the hard ground with considerable force.

'Never seen a red flapjack before,' mused Gimlet.

'There is my pledge of good faith,' Serutan went on smoothly. 'Do we have a deal?'

'No deals,' said Goodgulf. 'That knave is slipperier than a catfish in a jar of Vaseline.'

'Now wait,' said Arrowroot, 'he *did* pledge controlling interest.'

'N-O spells no,' said Goodgulf, adjusting his hat. 'I don't want to wake up some bright morning with his pledge between my shoulder blades.'

Just then a small black object whizzed past Goodgulf's head.

'This is getting monotonous,' Gimlet opined.

The round sphere bounced along the pavement and came to rest at Pepsi's toes. He looked at it curiously and picked it up.

'We will leave you under guard in your foul tower,' said Goodgulf, 'and the Vee-Ates will deal with you when your larder is empty of frozen cube steaks.'

Goodgulf turned and pointed to Pepsi.

'Okay, drop it.'

'Aw, I wasn't doing nothing,' said Pepsi.

'Yeah, nothing,' defended Moxie.

'Let me have it,' said the Wizard impatiently, 'you can't eat it, so you have no use for it.'

The young boggie handed the black ball over glumly.

'Now,' said Goodgulf, 'we must move quickly. Though the lands of Isinglass and Roi-Tan are safe from Serutan's power, they will not long be thus unless Twodor itself is saved from Sorhed's malevolence.'

'What must we do?' said Moxie.

'Yes, do?' asked Pepsi.

'If you'll belt up for a second I will tell thee,' Goodgulf snapped. 'The fair city of Minas Troney is threatened by Sorhed's eastern armies. The foul city of Chikken Noodul lies near, and any day the black cloud will fall upon her fairer sister. We must gather all our forces and defend her.' He beckoned Arrowroot. 'You, Stomper, must take it upon yourself to gather your subjects in Twodor and anyone else who will come to shore up the ramparts of Minas Troney. Eorache, you must bring all the riders you can spare and Birdseye too must lead his valiant Vee-Ates to Twodor. The rest will proceed with me there directly.'

'A hundred words without a punchline,' said Gimlet. 'The old crock must be sick.'

The party bade farewell and rode from the broken fortress of Isinglass with heavy heart, knowing that still more trouble would plague the land. Goodgulf, Moxie, and Pepsi mounted their complaining bleaters and spurred on in the evening shadows towards the fabled capital of Twodor. As they left, two fair young carrots waved their greens after the boggies and jumped hopefully up and down upon their dainty taproots, somewhat hindered by already noticeable swellings in their middles. Moxie and Pepsi had not been idle, since Goodgulf had seen them last.

All night and half the next day Goodgulf and the two boggies rode ever watchful for Sorhed's spies. Once overheard Moxie saw a black shape flapping eastward between the clouds and thought he heard a low, vile *croaking*. But he had been on pipeweed for several hours beforehand and wasn't sure.

Finally they rested. Goodgulf and Moxie conked off immediately after a quick game of craps (Moxie lost), and Pepsi, too, lay down as if in a deep snooze. But when his companions' snores became regular, he slowly slithered from his pup tent and rifled the Wizard's saddle bags. There he found the round, black ball Goodgulf had so carefully hidden.

It was smaller than a muskmelon, though larger than a pool ball. Its surface was featureless save for a small, circular window into the black interior.

'A magic wishing-ball!' he exclaimed. 'That's what it is.'

The boggie closed his eyes and wished for a keg of ale and a barrel of breaded veal cutlets. There was a small *foof* and a puff of fiery smoke, and Pepsi found himself staring into the face of a monstrous, unspeakably vile visage, its jowls quivering with malevolence and rage.

'I told you to keep your paws *off* of it!' shrieked the Wizard, his bell-bottoms flapping angrily.

'Aw, I was only looking at it,' Pepsi whined.

Goodgulf snatched the ball away from Pepsi and glowered. 'This,' he said harshly, 'is no plaything. This ball is the wondrous *mallomar*, the magic watchamacallit of the elves, long thought lost in the Sheet-Metal Age.'

'Why didn't you say so?' said Pepsi pointlessly.

'With *mallomar* the Old Ones probed the secrets of the future and looked deep into the hearts of men.'

'Sort of like a Ouija board?' said Moxie sleepily.

'Watch closely!' Goodgulf commanded.

The two boggies watched with interest as the wizard made mysterious passes over the sphere and muttered a weird incantation.

> *Hocus pocus*
> *Loco Parentis!*
> *Jackie Onassis*
> *Dino de Laurentiis!*

Before their frightened eyes the boggies saw the sphere glow. Goodgulf continued to mutter over it.

> *Queequeg quahog!*
> *Quodnam quixote!*
> *Pequod peapod!*
> *Pnin Peyote!*
> *Presto change-o*
> *Toil and trouble*
> *Rollo chunky*
> *Double-Bubble!*

Suddenly the globe seemed to burst from within with a sparkling radiance, and a quavering sound hummed through the air. Pepsi heard Goodgulf's voice through the shimmering glow.

'Tell me, O magic *mallomar*, shall Sorhed be defeated or shall he conquer? Shall the black cloud of Doom fall on all of Lower Middle Earth, or shall there be sunshine and happiness with his fall?'

Pepsi and Moxie were astonished to see fiery letters begin to form in the air, fiery letters that would foretell the fate of the coming struggle with Dark Lord. It was with wonder that they read the answer: *Reply Hazy, Ask Again Later.*

VIII

SCHLOB'S LAIR AND
OTHER MOUNTAIN RESORTS

Frito and Spam clambered out of breath to the top of a small rise and gazed out at the landscape that stretched before them, unbroken save for sudden depressions and swiftly rising gorges, to the slag mines, dress factories, and lint mills of Fordor. Frito sat down heavily on a cow's skull, and Spam produced a box lunch of cheese and crackers from their bags.

At that moment there came the sound of falling pebbles, stepped-on twigs, and a nose being violently blown. The two boggies leaped to their feet, and a gray, scaly creature crept slowly up to them on all fours, sniffing the ground noisily.

'Mother of pearl,' cried Frito, recoiling from the sinister figure. Spam drew his elvish pinking knife and stepped back, his heart in his mouth with the gooey glob of crackers.

The creature looked at them with ominously crossed eyes, and with a little smile, rose tiredly to its feet, and clasping its hands behind his back, began to whistle mournfully.

Suddenly Frito remembered Dildo's tale of the finding of the Ring.

'You must be Goddam!' he squeaked. 'What are you doing here?'

'Oh, well,' said the creature, speaking very slowly. 'Not much. I was just looking for a few old pop bottles to help pay for my sister-in-law's iron lung. Of course, ever since my operation I don't get around like I used to. Guess I'm just unlucky. Funny how life is, up and down, never can tell. Gosh, it sure is cold. I had to pawn my coat to buy plasma for my pet geese.'

Spam tried desperately to keep his leaden eyelids open, but with a great yawn, he slumped heavily to the ground. 'You fiend,' he muttered, and fell asleep.

'There I go again,' said Goddam, shaking his head. 'Well, I know when I'm not wanted,' he said, and sat down and helped himself to the boggies' elvish melba toast.

Frito slapped himself in the face several times and did a few deep breathing exercises.

'Look here, Goddam,' he said.

'Oh, you don't have to say it. Not wanted. I know. I never was. My mother left me in a twenty-four-hour locker in an enchanted forest when I was two. I was raised by kindly rats. But I guess every cloud has its silver lining. Why, I knew a troll once, name of Wyzinski . . .'

Frito swayed, drooped, and was snoring before he hit the ground. When Frito and Spam awoke, it was already night, and there was no sign of Goddam anywhere. Both boggies felt to make sure that they still had their original complement of fingers, legs, and the like, and that no cutlery had been inadvertently left in their ribs. To their considerable surprise, nothing was missing, not so much as a hangnail or a cufflink. Frito felt the Ring still securely fastened to its chain, and slipping it quickly on his finger, he blew through the magic whistle and was relieved to hear the familiar flat E.

'I don't get it, Mr Frito,' said Spam finally, feeling with his tongue for missing fillings, 'that one's a pigeon-fancier or worse.'

'Well, hello there,' said a large rock suddenly, becoming Goddam by degrees.

'Hello,' said Frito weakly.

'We were just leaving,' said Spam quickly. 'We have to close an arms deal in Tanzania or pick up some copra on Guam or something.'

'That's too bad,' said Goddam. 'I guess it's goodbye for old Goddam. But he's used to it.'

'Goodbye,' said Spam firmly.

'Goodbye, goodbye, parting is such a brief candle,' said Goddam. He waved a great stained handkerchief listlessly back and forth, and grasping Frito by the hand, began to sob softly.

Spam took hold of Frito's other arm and bodily dragged him away, but Goddam remained tightly attached, and after a minute or two, he gave up and sank exhausted on a rock.

'I hate to see an old friend go,' said Goddam, applying the handkerchief liberally over the cup custard he had by way of face. 'I'll just see you on your way.'

'Let's go,' said Frito dejectedly, and the three small figures set off at a quick pace across the hot-blooded moors.

Before long, they came to a place where the ground, well-watered by a vivid green stream, became damp and squishy, and Goddam slogged ahead of them. In a few hundred feet the way was completely blocked by a thick, fetid bog choked with well-smoked briars and lily cups.

'It is the Ngaio Marsh,' said Goddam solemnly, and Frito and Spam saw mysteriously reflected in the mucky pools eerie visions of bodies with ornate daggers in their backs, bullet holes in their heads, and poison bottles in their hands.

The little group plodded forward through the foul fen, averting their eyes from the grisly corpses, and after an hour of heavy going, they came, wet and filthy, to drier land. There they found a narrow path which led arrow-straight across an empty plain to a huge arrowhead. The moon had set, and dawn was coloring the sky a faint brown when they reached the curiously shaped rock.

Frito and Spam dropped their bags under a little ledge, and Goddam settled down behind them, humming a gum jingle.

'Well, we're right in the old ballpark,' he said, almost cheerily.

Frito groaned.

The boggies were awakened in the late afternoon by the clash of cymbals and the harsh sound of trumpets playing 'Busman's Holiday.' Frito and Spam sprang to their feet and saw, frighteningly close, the great Gate of Fordor set into the high mountain wall. The gate itself, flanked by two tall towers topped with search lights and a vast marquee, lay open, and an enormous line of men was pouring in. Frito shrank back in fear against the rock.

It was night before the last of the hordes had passed into Fordor, and the Gate had closed with a deep clang. Spam peeped out from behind a stone outcropping and slipped over to Frito with a frugal meal of loaves and fishes. Goddam immediately appeared from a narrow crevice and smiled obscenely.

'The way to a man's heart is through his stomach,' he said.

'That's just what I've been thinking,' said Spam, fingering the hilt of his sword.

Goddam looked mournful. 'I know how it is,' he said. 'I was in the war. Pinned down in a deadly hail of Jap fire . . .'

Spam gagged, and his arm went limp. 'Die,' he suggested.

Frito took a large loaf of raisin bread and crammed it into Goddam's mouth.

'Mmmmf, mfffl, mmblgl,' said the beast darkly.

The little party set out once more into the night and walked for many long liters into the south, always skirting the stony ring that surrounded Fordor with a ring of stone. The road they followed was flat and smooth, the remnant of some ancient linoleum-paved highway, and by the time the moon was high in the sky, they had left the Gate of Fordor far behind. Around midnight the stars became obscured with a great many clouds the size of a man's hand, and shortly after a tremendous torrent swept through the land, pouring wet, annoyed pointers and retrievers on the miserable travelers. But the boggies pressed on behind Goddam, and after a bruising fifteen minutes, the storm passed and, dropping a few last chihuahuas, moved westward.

For the rest of the night they journeyed under dimly visible stars, numbed by the cold and Goddam's endless stream of knock-knock jokes. It was very late at night when they found themselves at the edge of a large forest, and heading off the road, they took shelter in a small grove. In a moment they were fast asleep.

Frito awoke with a start to find the little grove completely surrounded by tall, grim-looking men clad from head to toe in British racing green. They held huge green bows, and they wore shaggy wigs of bright green hair. Frito rose unsteadily to his feet and kicked Spam.

At that point, the tallest of the bowmen stepped forward and approached him. He wore a propeller beanie with a long green feather and a large silver badge with the word *Chief* and some recumbent pigeons, and Frito guessed that he must be their leader.

'You're completely surrounded; you haven't got a chance; come out with your hands up,' said the captain sternly.

Frito bowed low. 'Come in and get me,' he said, making the correct reply.

'I am Farahslax, of the Green Toupées,' said the captain.

'I am Frito, of nothing in particular,' said Frito shakily.

'Can I kill them a little?' squealed a short squat man with a black nose-patch, rushing to Farahslax with a garrote.

'Nay, Magnavox,' said Farahslax. 'Who are you?' he said, turning to Frito, 'and what is your evil purpose?'

'My companions and I are going to Fordor to cast the Great Ring into the Zazu Pits,' said Frito.

At this, Farahslax's face darkened, and looking first at Goddam and Spam, then back to Frito, he tiptoed out of the grove with a little smile and disappeared with his men into the surrounding forest, singing merrily:

>*We are stealthy Green Toupées*
>*Skulking nights and snoozing days,*
>*A team of silent, nasty men,*
>*Who all think Sorhed's numbah ten.*

>>*Draw their fire*
>>*Flank on right*
>>*Narcs retire*
>>*Fight-team-fight!*

>*Using every grungy trick*
>*From booby trap to pungee stick*
>*We hardly need the strength of thirty*
>*When we can win by playing dirty.*

>>*Two-four-six-eight*
>>*Tiptoe, sneak*
>>*And infiltrate*
>>*Cha-cha-cha.*

It was not many hours before night when the green men left, and after a leisurely meal of apple cheeks and cauliflower ears, Frito, Spam, and Goddam returned to the high road and passed quickly out of the forest and into the wide asphalt waste that lay beneath the eastern slope of Fordor. By nightfall they had come under the shadow of the black chimneys of Chikken Noodul, the dread company town that stood across from Minas Troney. From deep within the earth came the heavy *whomp-whomp* of fell engines producing overshoes and mess kits for Sorhed's war machine.

Goddam led Frito and Spam through the brown gloom to a fin-worn salmon ladder that led sharply up into the heavy mass of the Sol Hurok, the great cliffs of Fordor. They climbed for what seemed like an hour. An hour later they reached the top, exhausted and gagging on the heavy air, and flung themselves down on a narrow ledge at the mouth of a great cavern overlooking the black vale.

Above them wheeled huge flocks of black pelicans, and all around them lightning flashed and graves yawned and fell asleep.

'Things look black, and no mistake,' said Spam.

A pungent smell of old pastrami and rancid gherkins floated out of the cave, and from deep within some hidden chamber came the sinister click of knitting needles.

Frito and Spam walked warily into the tunnel, and Goddam shuffled after them, a rare smile playing across his face.

Ages ago when the world was young and Sorhed's heart had not yet hardened like stale cheesecake, he had taken a young troll-maiden as his wife. Her name was Mazola, called by the elves Blanche, and she married the handsome young witch-king over the objections of her parents, who pointed out that Sorhed 'simply wasn't trollish' and could never provide for her special needs. But the two were young and starry-eyed. The first hundred thousand years found the newlyweds still quite happy; they then lived in a converted three-room dungeon with a view, and while the ambitious hubby studied demonology and business administration at night school, Mazola bore him nine strapping wraiths.

Then came the day when Sorhed learned of the Great Ring and the many powers it would bring him in his climb to the top. Forgetting all else, he yanked his sons from medical school over his wife's strident objections and dubbed then Nozdruls. But the First Ring War went badly. Sorhed and his Ringers barely escaped with their lives. From then on their marital relations went from bad to worse. Sorhed spent all his time at the witch-works and Mazola sat home casting evil spells and watching the daytime *mallomar* serials.

She began to put on weight. Then, one day, Sorhed found Mazola and a *mallomar* repairman in a compromising position and immediately filed divorce proceedings, eventually winning custody of the Nine Nozdrul.

Mazola, now banished to her drab surroundings in the bowels of Sol Hurok, let her hatred grow and fester. Schlob, was she now called. For eons she nurtured her pique, obsessively stuffing herself with bon-bons, movie magazines, and an occasional spelunker. At first, Sorhed dutifully sent her monthly alimony payments of a dozen or so narc volunteers, but these gifts soon stopped when word got around what a dinner invitation with Sorhed's ex actually entailed. Her gnawing fury knew no bounds. She prowled her lair with murderous intent, eternally cursing the memory of her husband and his derisive trolack jokes. For ages her only interest had been revenge as she brooded in her dark, dark lair. Cutting off her lights had been the last straw.

Frito and Spam now descended into the bowels of Sol Hurok with Goddam right behind them. Or so they assumed. Deeper and deeper they plunged into the dark heavy vapors of the cavernous passageways, tripping continually on piles of skulls and rotting treasure chests. With unseeing eyes they searched through the blackness.

'Sure is dark, I'm a-thinkin',' whispered Spam.

'Brilliant observation,' shushed Frito. 'Are you sure this is the right way, Goddam?'

There was no answer.

'Must have gone on ahead,' Frito said hopefully.

A long time they inched their way forward through the murky tunnels. Frito clutched the ring tightly. He heard a faint *squishing* noise ahead in the tunnel. Frito stopped in his tracks, and since Spam had hold of his tail, they fell with a clatter that echoed and re-echoed loudly through the black spaces. The *squishing* subsided, then grew louder. And closer.

'Back the other way,' rasped Frito, 'and quickly!'

The boggies fled the ominous *squishing* down many twists and turns, but it was still gaining on them, and the sickening odor of stale bon-bons filled the air. They ran blindly on until a great commotion before them blocked further escape.

'Look out,' whispered Frito, 'it's a patrol of narcs.'

Spam soon knew that this was so, for their foul tongues and clanking armor were unmistakable. They were, as usual, disputing and cracking filthy jokes as they approached. Frito and Spam flattened themselves against the wall, hoping to escape unseen.

'Cripes,' hissed a voice in the dark, 'this place always give me the creeps!'

'Nuts to you,' lashed back another, 'the lookout says that boggie with the Ring is in here.'

'Yeah,' opined a third, 'and if we don't get it Sorhed'll break us back down to nightmares.'

'Third class,' agreed a fourth.

The narcs grew closer and the boggies held their breath as they passed. Just as Frito thought they had passed, a cold, slimy hand clutched his chest.

'Hoo boy!' exulted the narc. 'I got 'em, I got 'em!'

In a trice the narcs were upon them with billyclubs and handcuffs.

'Sorhed will be pleased to see you two!' cackled a narc, pressing his face (and breath) close to Frito's.

All at once a great, guttural moan shivered the dark tunnel and the narcs fell back in terror.

'Crud!' a narc screamed. 'It's her nibs!'

'Schlob! Schlob!' wailed another, lost in the darkness.

Frito drew Tweezer from its scabbard, but could see nothing to strike. Thinking quickly, he remembered the magic snowglobe given him by Lavalier. Holding the glass at arm's length, he hopefully pressed the little button on the bottom. Immediately a blinding carbon arc-light flooded the dank surroundings, revealing a vast chamber of formica paneling and cheap chintz. And there, before them, was the terrible bulk of Schlob.

Spam cried out at the sight most horrible to behold. She was a huge, shapeless mass of quivering flesh. Her flame-red eyes glowered as she slogged forward to the narcs, her tatty print shift dragged on the stone floor. Falling upon her fear-frozen victims with her fat body, she ripped them apart with taloned house slippers and sharp fangs dripping great yellow droplets of chicken soup.

'Wash behind your ears!' Schlob shrieked as she tore a narc limb from limb and discarded his armor like a candy wrapper.

'You never take me anywhere!' she foamed, popping the wriggling torso into her maw. 'The best years of my life I gave you!' she raged, her sharp red fingernails reaching out for the boggies.

Frito stepped back against the wall and slashed at the greedy nails with Tweezer, only managing to chip the enamel. Schlob squealed, further enraged. As the ravenous creature closed in, Frito's last memory was of Spam frantically schpritzing insect repellent into Schlob's bottomless gullet.

IX

MINAS TRONEY IN THE SOUP

The evening sun was setting, as is its wont, in the west as Goodgulf, Moxie, and Pepsi reined in their exhausted merinos at the gates of Minas Troney. The boggies were dazzled by the fabled capital of all Twodor, Stronghold of the West and Lower Middle Earth's largest producer of crude oil, yo-yos, and emery wheels. Surrounding the townlands were the Plains of Pellegranor, whose earth was rich with many an oast and garner, not to mention wide tilths, folds, byres, rippling rilns, and rolling ferndocks. The desultory Effluvium washed these green lands and year after year provided the ingrate residents with bumper crops of salamanders and anopheles mosquitoes. It was little wonder that the city drew multitudes of pointed-headed Southrons, thick-lipped Northrons, and inverted Ailerons. It was the only place where they could get a passport out of Twodor.

The city itself dated back to the Olden Days when Beltelephon the Senile decreed rather inexplicably that there be built in this flat land a royal ski lodge of wondrous beauty. Unfortunately the old King cashed in before he saw ground broken and his hydrocephalic son, Nibasco the Incompetent, typically misread the late codger's vague blueprints and ordered somewhat more prestressed concrete than necessary for the original design. The result was Minas Troney or 'Nabisco's Folly.'

For no good reason, the city was made in seven concentric circles topped with a commemorative double statue of Beltelephon and his favourite concubine, whose name was either Nephritis the Obese or Phyllis. In any case the final architectural effect was that of an Italian wedding cake.* Each ring was higher than the next, as were the rents. In the lowest, seventh ring dwelt the city's sturdy yeomen. Oft they could be seen dutifully polishing their brightly colored yeos for some idiotic festival or other. In the sixth ring dwelt tradesmen, warriors in the fifth, and so on to the first and highest level, wherein dwelt the Great Stewards and dentists. Each level was reached by means of wind-powered escalators in constant need of repair so that the social climber of these ancient times was just that. Each ring was proud of its own history and showed its scorn of that beneath it by daily bombardments of refuse, and expressions such as 'Let's go seventhing' and 'Dahling, don't be so third-level' were

* The historian Bocaraton notes that this may have been intentionally 'emblematic of the crumbs inside.'

common.* Each level was obliquely protected by out-thrusting battlements corniced and groined at the odd enjambments. Each odd enjambment was set perpendicular to every even adjacent one-way thoroughfare. Needless to say, the inhabitants were always late for their appointments, if not totally lost.

As the three slowly wound their way toward the Palace of Benelux the Steward, the citizens of Twodor gaped at them briefly and walked immediately to their nearest optometrist. Curiously the boggies stared back at the dwellers: men, elves, dwarves, banshees, and not a few Republicans were among them.

'Any convention burg gets a pretty mixed bag,' Goodgulf explained.

Slowly they ascended the last, creaking set of moving steps and alighted at the first level. Pepsi rubbed his eyes at the edifice before him. It was of lavish design with broad lawns and sumptuous gardens. Rich marble paved the path beneath their feet, and the tinkling of many fountains sang like silver coins. At the door they were rather rudely informed that the dentist was not at home and they-must-be-looking-for-the-old-coot-round-back.

There they found a run-down palace wrought of stoutest Masonite, its walls aglow with fiery inlays of

* It is not known upon whom the refuse of the lowest ring was thrown, but it is conjectured that it was not thrown at all, but eaten.

rock candy and old bicycle reflectors. Over the re-inforced plywood door was a sign reading THE STEWARD IS OUT. Beneath that there was another announcing OUT TO LUNCH, and beneath that, GONE FISHING.

'Benelux must not be here, if I read these signs aright,' said Moxie.

'I think it's a bluff,' said Goodgulf as he rang the bell insistently, 'for the Stewards of Minas Troney have always been private in their ways. Benelux the Booby, son of Electrolux the Piker, comes from a long line of Stewards dating back many arid generations. Long have they ruled Twodor. The first Great Steward, Parrafin the Climber, was employed in King Chloroplast's kitchen as second scullery boy when the old King met a tragic death. He apparently fell backward by accident on a dozen salad forks. Simultan-eously the true heir, his son Carotene, mysteriously fled the city, complaining of some sort of plot and a lot of threatening notes left on his breakfast tray. At the time, this looked suspicious what with his father's death, and Carotene was suspected of foul play. Then the rest of the King's relatives began to drop dead one after the other in an odd fashion. Some were found strangled with dishrags and some succumbed to food poisoning. A few were found drowned in the soup vats, and one was attacked by assailants unknown and beaten to death with a pot roast. At least three appear to have thrown themselves backward on salad forks, perhaps in a noble gesture of grief over the King's untimely end. Finally there was no one left in Minas Troney who was either eligible or willing to wear the accursed crown, and the rule of Twodor was up for grabs. The scullery slave Parrafin bravely accepted the Stewardship of Twodor until that day when a lineal descendant of Carotene's returns to reclaim his rightful throne, conquer Twodor's enemies, and revamp the postal system.'

Just then a peephole in the door opened and a beady eye inspected them.

'W-w-what you want?' the voice demanded.

'We are wayfarers here to aid the fortunes of Minas Troney. I am Goodgulf Grayteeth.' The Wizard took a crumpled slip of paper from his wallet and handed it through the hole.

'W-what this?'

'My card,' replied Goodgulf. It returned immediately in a dozen pieces.

'Steward not home. On vacation. N-n-no p-peddlers!' The peephole closed with a small slam.

But Goodgulf was not easily duped and the boggies could tell from his eyes that he was angered by this impudence. His pupils were crossing and uncrossing like a juggler's oranges. He rang again, long and loud.

The eye blinked at them and a smell of garlic floated from the hole.

'Y-you again? Told you, he's t-t-taking a shower.' Again the hole shut.

Goodgulf said nothing. He reached into his Mao jacket and extracted a black ball that Pepsi at first thought was the *mallomar* with a string attached. Goodgulf lit it with the end of his cigar and tossed the ball unto the mail slot. He then ran around the corner with the boggies in tow. There was a large *boom* and, when the boggies peeked around to look, the door had magically disappeared.

Pridefully the three walked through the smoking portals. They were confronted by a seedy old palace guard who was wiping the soot from his smarting eyes.

'You may tell Benelux that Goodgulf the Wizard awaits an audience.'

The doddering warrior bowed resentfully and led them through the airless passageways.

'T-t-the S-steward isn't going t-to like t-this,' croaked the guard. 'H-h-hasn-'t been out of p-p-palace for years.'

'Do not the people grow restive?' asked Pepsi.

'T-their idea,' drooled the old guide.

He led them through an armorial hall whose cardboard arches and plaster-of-paris vaultings towered fully a foot over their heads. Richly mimeographed tapestries depicted past Kings' legendary deeds. Pepsi particularly liked one about a long-dead king and a she-goat and said so. Goodgulf smacked him one. The very walls glittered with inset ginger-ale bottles and costume jewelry, and the polished aluminum armor cast brilliant reflections on the hand-laid linoleum at their feet.

At last they came to the throne room with its fabled thumb-tack mosaics. By the looks of the place the Royal Throne Room gave double service as the Royal Shower Room. The guard disappeared and was replaced by an equally aged page in olive-drab livery. He struck a brass dinner gong and rasped:

'Cringe and scrape thee before Benelux, Great Steward of Twodor, true regent of the Lost King who will one day return or so they say.'

The hoary page ducked around a screen and a curtain fluttered nearby. Out rolled the wizened Benelux in a battered wheelchair drawn by a brace of puffing raccoons. He wore tuxedo trousers, a short red jacket, and a clip-on bow tie. On his balding head rested a chauffeur's cap emblazoned with the Crest of the Stewards, a rather showy affair featuring a winged unicorn carrying a tea tray. Moxie caught a distinct whiff of garlic.

Goodgulf cleared his throat, for the Steward was obviously sound asleep.

'Greetings and Happy Holidays,' he began. 'I am Goodgulf, Court Wizard to the Crowned Heads of Lower Middle Earth, Worker of Wonders and Certified Chiropractor.'

The old Steward opened one coated eye and looked at Moxie and Pepsi with disgust.

'W-w-what are those? Sign at door says "no pets." '

'They are boggies, my liege, small yet trusty allies of ours to the north.'

'I'll have g-g-guard spread some papers,' the Steward mumbled as his wrinkled head fell heavily to his chest.

Goodgulf *ahemed* and continued.

'I fear that I am the bearer of dark tidings and sad. Sorhed's foul narcs have slain thy own beloved son Bromosel and now the Dark Lord wishes thy own life and thy realm for his own unspeakable designs.'

'Bromosel?' said the Steward, rousing himself on one elbow.

'Thy own beloved son,' prompted Goodgulf.

A flicker of recognition passed through tired old eyes.

'Oh, him. Never w-w-writes except for m-money. Just l-like the other one. T-too bad about t-t-that.'

'Thus we have come with an army a few days' ride behind to revenge your grief upon Fordor,' Goodgulf explained.

The Steward waved his feeble hands with annoyance.

'Fordor? N-n-never heard of it. No two-bit w-w-wizard n-neither. Audience over,' said the Steward.

'Insult not the White Wizard,' warned Goodgulf as he drew something from his pocket, 'for I have many powers. Here, pick a card. Any card.'

Benelux selected one of the fifty-two sevens of hearts and tore it into confetti. 'Audience over,' he repeated with finality.

'Foolish dotard,' growled Goodgulf later in their room at an inn. He had been fussing and fuming for over an hour.

'But what can we do if he will not help us?' asked Moxie. 'The bird is nutty as an elf-cake.'

Goodgulf snapped his fingers as if an idea had dawned in his sly head.

'That's it!' he chuckled. 'The old prune is known to be mental.'

'So are his pals,' observed Pepsi sagely.

'Psychotic too,' mused the Wizard. 'I bet he's got a lot of suicidal psychoses. Self-destructive. Textbook case.'

'Suicidal?' said Pepsi with surprise. 'How do you say that?'

'It's just a hunch,' Goodgulf replied distantly, 'just a hunch.'

The news of the Old Steward's suicide that evening stirred the city. The tabloids ran a large photograph of the burning pyre into which he leapt after first ingeniously tying himself up and writing a final farewell to his subjects. Headlines that day screamed BATTY BENELUX BURNS and later editions reported WIZARD LAST TO SEE STEWARD: CITES SORHED AS CAUSE OF B.'S TORMENT. Since Benelux's entire staff had mysteriously disappeared, Goodgulf generously took it upon himself to arrange a State Funeral and proclaim a Lunch Hour of National Mourning for the fallen ruler. During the next few days of confusion and political turmoil the persuasive Wizard serenely held numerous press conferences. By the hour he conferred with high officials to explain that it was his old friend's last wish that he, Goodgulf, hold the reins of government until his surviving son, Farahslax, returned. In unguarded moments he could be found in the palace's executive washroom trying to scour out a faint smell of garlic and kerosene.

Within a remarkably short time, Goodgulf had galvanized the sleepy capital into a drilling militia. Marshaling Minas Troney's resources, the Wizard personally drew up ration lists, fortification plans, and lucrative defense contracts which he himself filled. At first there was a clamor of protest against Goodgulf's extraordinary powers. But then an angry black cloud began growing over the city. This, plus a few un-explained explosions in Opposition newspaper offices, silenced 'those damned isolationists,' as Goodgulf dubbed them in a widely publicized interview. Soon after, stragglers from the eastern provinces told of hordes of narcs attacking and overwhelming Twodor's border outpost at Ohmigoshgolli. Soon, Twodor knew, Sorhed's dogs would be sniffing at the city's very pants cuffs.

Moxie and Pepsi fidgeted impatiently in the waiting room of Goodgulf's palace offices, their feet dangling a foot or so short of the plush carpet. Although proud of their new uniforms (Goodgulf had commissioned the pair as Twodorian lieutenant colonels), the boggies had seen little of the Wizard, and the rumor of narcs had made them mickle itchy.

'Can't he see us now?' whined Pepsi.

'We've been waiting for hours!' added Moxie.

The shapely elf-receptionist shifted the torques in her clinging blouse indifferently.

'I'm sorry,' she said for the eighth time that morning, 'but the wizard is still in conference.'

The bell on her desk rang, and before she could

cover the speaking tube, the boggies heard Goodgulf's voice.

'Are they gone yet?'

The elf-maiden reddened as the boggies bolted past her and through the door to Goodgulf's office. There they found the Wizard with a fat cigar between his teeth and a pair of bleached-blond sylphs perched on his bony knees. He looked at Pepsi and Moxie with annoyance.

'Can't you see I'm busy?' he snapped. 'In conference. Very important.' Goodgulf made as if to resume his conference.

'Not so fast,' said Pepsi.

'Yeah, fast,' Moxie emphasized, helping himself to the dish of black caviar on Goodgulf's desk.

Goodgulf made a deep sigh and bade the languid sylphs withdraw.

'Well, well,' Goodgulf said with strained affability, 'what can I do for you?'

'Not as much as you seem to have done for yourself,' said Moxie with a black-smudged grin.

'Can't complain,' Goodgulf replied. 'Fortune has smiled upon me. Help yourself to my lunch.' Moxie had just finished it and was going through Goodgulf's drawers for more.

'We grow fearful,' said Pepsi as he plunked himself down in an expensive troll-hide chair. 'Rumors run through the city of narcs and other foul fiends approaching from the east. A black cloud has appeared over our heads and utilities are down eight and a half.'

Goodgulf blew a fat blue smoke ring.

'These are not matters for small ones,' he said. 'Besides, you're stealing my lines.'

'But the black cloud?' Pepsi asked.

'Just a few smudgepots I planted in the Knockon Wood. Keeps the folk hereabouts on their toes.'

'And the rumors of invaders?' said Moxie.

'Simply that,' said Goodgulf. 'Sorhed will not attack Minas Troney for a while yet, and by then the rest of our company will have brought reinforcements to the city.'

'Then there is no danger yet?' sighed Pepsi.

'Trust me,' said Goodgulf as he ushered them out the door. 'Wizards know many things.'

The surprise attack at dawn the next day caught everyone in Minas Troney by surprise. None of the planned fortifications had been completed, and the materials and men that were ordered and paid for through Goodgulf's office had never appeared. In the night a vast horde had completely surrounded the fair city and their black encampments covered the green plains like a week-old scab. Black flags with the Red Nose of Sorhed fluttered all about the city. Then, as the first rays of the sun touched the land, the black army assailed the walls.

Hundreds of narcs, their minds aflame with cheap muscatel, threw themselves at the gates. Behind them tramped companies of renegade trolls and rogue pandas, slavering with hate. Whole brigades of psychotic banshees and goblins raised their shrill voices in a loathsome war cry. At their rear marched niblicks and vicious mashies who could lay low many a brave Twodorian with a single stroke of their deadly meat tenderizers. From over a rise appeared a bloodthirsty mass of clerk-typists and the entire June Taylor Dancers. A sight most horrible to behold.

This, Goodgulf, Moxie, and Pepsi watched from the walls. The boggies were much afraid.

'They are so many and we are so few!' Pepsi cried, much afraid.

'True heart is the strength of ten,' said Goodgulf.

'We are so few and they are so many!' cried Moxie, afraid much.

'A watched pot never boils; whistle a happy tune,' observed Goodgulf. 'Too many cooks spoil the brouhaha.'

Reassured, the boggies donned their greaves, corslets, gauntlets, and shoulder padding and slathered themselves with Bactine. Each was armed with a double-edged putty knife, its blade both keen and true. Goodgulf wore an old deep-sea diver's suit of stoutest latex. Only the well-trimmed beard was recognizable through the helmet's little round window. In his hand he carried an ancient and trusty weapon, called by the elves a Browning semi-automatic.

Pepsi glimpsed a shadow above them and screamed. There was a *swooping* sound and all three ducked just in time. A laughing Nozdrul pulled his killer-pelican out of his power dive. The sky was suddenly full of the black birds, each piloted by a begoggled Black Rider. The marauders flapped hither and thither, taking aerial photographs and strafing hospitals, orphanages, and churches with guano. As they wheeled above the terrified city the pelicans opened their fanged maws to disgorge blank propaganda leaflets down upon the illiterate defenders.

But the Twodorians were harassed not only from above. Land forces were now battering the main gate and toppling men from the ramparts with flaming matzoh balls and the collected works of Rod McKuen. The very air was alive with the whizzing of poisoned boomerangs and high-velocity Dog Yummies. Several of the latter dented Goodgulf's helmet, giving him a near-fatal migraine.

All at once the front ranks parted before the walls and the boggies cried out with astonishment. A monstrous black peccary galloped to the gate. Its rider was the Lord of the Nozdrul. He was dressed all in black; great tire chains hung from his leather jacket. The huge wraith dismounted his tusker, his engineer boots sinking deep in the hard ground. Moxie caught a glimpse of a grotesque, pimpled face; the fiend's fangs and greasy sideburns flashed wetly in the noonday sun. The lord leered evilly at the ramparts of Twodorians, then lifted a black penny-whistle to a gaping nostril to sneeze a single, ear-splitting *blatt*.

Immediately a squad of gremlins half-crazed by cough syrup trundled out a huge female dragon on black roller skates. The rider patted its horned snout and climbed on its scaly back, directing the attention of the beast's single bloodshot eye upon the portal. The huge reptile nodded and rubber-legged on its wheels toward the wooden gate. Horrified, the Twodorians saw the Nozdrul ignite the dragon's pilot light; he spurred the monster's flanks and the torrent of fiery propane belched from its open jaws. The wall burst into flame and crumbled into ashes. Narcs eagerly hopped over the licking tongues and poured into the city.

'All is lost!' Moxie sobbed. He prepared to throw himself off the wall.

'Despair not,' Goodgulf commanded through his little window. 'Bring me my white robes, and quickly!'

'Ah!' cried Pepsi, 'white robes for white magic!'

'No,' said Goodgulf as he stapled the garments to a pool cue, 'white robes for white flag.'

Just as the Wizard was waving his robes in frantic semaphore, the sound of a hundred horns was heard in the west, answered by as many in the east. A great wind clove the black cloud and dispersed it, revealing through the parting mists a great shield bearing the words CAUTION: CIGARETTE SMOKING MAY BE HAZARDOUS TO YOUR HEALTH; the rocks split, and the sky, though cloudless, thundered like a thousand stagehands striking a thousand metal sheets. There was a release of pigeons.

From all points of the compass the joyful Twodorians saw great armies approaching with marching bands, fireworks, and showers of colored streamers. To the north was Gimlet leading a band of a thousand dwarves, to the south the familiar pronged bulk of Eorache in command of three thousand berserk *Sheepers*; from the east appeared two great armies, one of Farahslax's seasoned Green Toupées and one of Legolam's manned by four thousand sharp-nailed interior decorators. Lastly, from the west, rode gray-clad Arrowroot leading a party of four warbadgers and a cranky Cub Scout.

In a trice the armies converged on the embattled city and set upon the panicking enemy. The battle raged as the trapped attackers were mowed down with sword and club. Terrified trolls fled the murderous Roi-Tanner hooves only to be hewn to pieces by the dwarves' picks and shovels. The bodies of narcs and banshees littered the ground and the Lord of the Nozdrul was encircled by piqued elves who scratched out his eyes and pulled his hair until he fell on his own sword in embarrassment. The black pelicans and their Nozdrul pilots were pecked from the air by anti-aircraft gulls and the dragon was cornered by the Cub Scout and peppered with rubber-tipped arrows until it suffered a complete nervous breakdown and collapsed with a heavy *thud*.

Meanwhile, the heartened Twodorians rushed from the walls and flew at the fiends yet inside the city. Moxie and Pepsi drew their putty knives and wielded them deftly. Soon, not a fallen corpse had a nose to call his own. Goodgulf busied himself throttling narcs from behind with his rubber air hose and Arrowroot was very probably doing something or other that was pretty much brave. When later questioned about the battle, however, he usually went rather vague.

At last all the enemy were slain, and the few who managed to break through the deadly ring of soldiers were run down and quickly dispatched with a blow from a Roi-Tanner dustmop. The narcs' bodies were collected into large mounds. Goodgulf then merrily instructed that they be individually gift-wrapped and mailed to Fordor. C.O.D. The Twodorians began hosing down the stained ramparts and the still-quivering bulk of the dragon was carted off to the Royal Kitchens for that evening's victory feast.

But all was not well with Twodor. Many good men and true had fallen: the brothers Handlebar and Hersheybar, and Eorache's uncle, the trusty Eordrum. Dwarves and elves had their losses, and the sad whines of mourning mixed with the cheers of victory.

Though the leaders happily gathered for greeting, not even these were spared grievous hurt. Farahslax, son of Benelux and brother to Bromosel, had lost four toes and suffered a gash across the tummy. The fair Eorache was cut upon her massive biceps and both her monocles had been brutally smashed. Moxie and Pepsi lost a bit of their right earlobes in the fray, and Legolam's left pinky was severely sprained. Gimlet's pointed head had been somewhat flattened out by a mashie's tenderizer, but the flayed skin he now wore as a mackintosh attested to the outcome of that particular duel. Lastly limped Goodgulf, supported by the miraculously unscathed Ranger. The old Wizard's white bell-bottoms had been viciously frayed and there was a nasty stain on the front of his Nehru jacket; his go-go boots were beyond hope. He also wore his right arm in a matching sling, but when he later tended to switch it from arm to arm this wound was taken rather less seriously.

Tears flowed like water as they greeted each other. Even Gimlet and Legolam managed to limit their enmity to an obscene gesture or two. There was much laughing and embracing, particularly between Arrowroot and Eorache. Arrowroot, however, was not blind to certain glances that were exchanged when the *Scheepess* was introduced to the husky Farahslax.

'And this hero,' said Goodgulf at last to Arrowroot, 'is the brave Farahslax, true heir to the Stewardship of Twodor.'

'Charmed, I'll warrant,' replied Arrowroot icily as he simultaneously shook the warrior's hand and stepped on his wounded foot. 'I am Arrowroot of Arrowshirt, true son of Araplane and *true King of all Twodor*. You have already met fair Eorache, *my fiancée and Queen!*' The emphasis the Ranger put into his formal greeting was lost on no one.

'Greetings and salutations,' returned the Green Toupée. 'May your reign and marriage be as long as your life.' He crushed Arrowroot's hand as he shook it.

The two stared at each other with unabashed hatred.

'Let us all go to the House o' Healing,' said Arrowroot finally as he inspected his mangled fingers, 'for there are many wounds that I would heal.'

By the time the company had reached the palace much had been said. Goodgulf was roundly congratulated for

giving the attack signal with his flag. Many wondered at
his wisdom in knowing that help was on its way, but
on this matter the Wizard kept strangely silent. The
company also was saddened that Birdseye could not
share their victory this day, for the green giant and his
trusty Vee-Ates had been most foully ambushed on the
way back from Isinglass by a black herd of Sorhed's
wraith-rabbits. Of the once-mighty army not even a
single stalk remained. Moxie and Pepsi shed bitter tears
for the loss of their fecund carrots and danced a little jig
of despair.

'And now,' said Arrowroot, beckoning the
wounded warriors to a concrete bunker, 'let us retire
to yon . . . er . . . House o' Healing, where we may
purge our troubles.' He looked pointedly at Farahslax.

'Healing-schmealing, ve ist hokay,' objected Eorache, looking at Farahslax like a dog gloating over a
pound of minute steak.

'Heed my words,' Arrowroot commanded, stomping a boot.

The company protested feebly, but obeyed so as not
to hurt his feelings. There, Arrowroot donned a white
apron and a plastic stethoscope and ran hither and yon
seeing after the patients. He put Farahslax in a private
room far from the others.

'Nothing but the best for the Steward of Twodor,'
he explained.

Soon all were tended to, save the new Steward. Arrowroot allowed that Farahslax had had a relapse in his private room and an operation was immediately necessary. He would meet them at the victory feast later.

The feast in the main cafeteria of Benelux's palace was a sight to behold. Goodgulf had unearthed great stores of delicacies; the same delicacies, it happened, as those that were earlier placed on the Wizard's ration lists. Yards of twisted crêpe paper and glowing fold-up lanterns bedazzled the guests' eyes. Goodgulf himself hired the two-piece all-troll orchestra to serenade the diners from a low dais of old orange crates, and all drank largely from the kegs of rotgut mead. Then the guests, plastered elves, drunk dwarves, reeling men, and a few schnozzled unidentifiables staggered with their brimming trays to the long banquet table and began gobbling as if it were their last meal.

'Not as dumb as they look,' Goodgulf blearily observed to Legolam at his left.

The Wizard, brilliantly attired in fresh bell-bottoms, slumped at the head of the table with the stinkoed boggies, Legolam, Gimlet, and Eorache in the folding chairs of honor. Only the absence of Farahslax and Arrowroot stayed the official proceedings.

'Where d'ya sh'pose they are?' Moxie asked finally above the clatter of trays and plastic flagons.

Moxie's question was answered, or at least half answered, as the swinging doors of the banquet hall flew open and a bloodstained, disheveled figure appeared.

'Shtomper!' cried Pepsi.

The hundreds of guests paused in their repast. Before them stood Arrowroot, still in his apron, covered mask to boot with gore. One hand was swathed in bandages and he bore a nasty-looking mouse under one eye.

'Vas ist?' said Eorache. 'Where ist der handsome Farahslaxer?'

'Alas,' the Ranger sighed, 'Farahslax is no more. I tried mightily to heal his wounds, but it was in vain. His hurts were many and sore.'

'Vhat vas der matter mit him?' sobbed the Roi-Tanner. 'He vas fine vhen ve left.'

'Terminal abrasions and contusions,' said Arrowroot, sighing again, 'with complications. His cuticles were completely severed, poor soul. Never had a chance.'

'I could have sworn he didn't have more than a bump on hish head,' muttered Legolam under the cover of his sleeve.

'Aye,' replied Arrowroot, shooting the elf a withering glance, 'so it might seem to one unschooled in the art of healing. But that bump, that fatal bump, 'twas his downfall. 'Twas water on the brain. 'Tis ninety-percent fatal. Forced I was to amputate. Sad, very sad.'

Arrowroot strode to his folding chair, his face lined with care. As if by some prearranged signal some disreputable-looking Brownies leapt to their feet and shouted, 'The last Steward is no more! All hail Arrowroot of Arrowshirt, King of Twodor hail!'

Stomper touched his hatbrim in humble acknowl-edgment of Twodor's new allegiance, and Eorache, seeing which way the wind was blowing, threw her brawny arms around the new King with a creditable squeal of delight. The rest of the guests, either confused or drunk, echoed the cheers with a thousand voices.

But then, from the back of the chamber, a shrill, piping voice was heard.

'Nay! Nay!' it squeaked.

Arrowroot searched the table and the dizzy crowd grew silent. At the very end was a squat figure wear-ing a black nosepatch, dressed all in green. It was Magnavox, friend to the late Farahslax.

'Speak,' commanded Arrowroot, hoping he wouldn't.

'If you be the true King of Twodor,' Magnavox

fluted drunkenly, 'you will fulfil the propheshy and deshtroy our enemiesh. Thish you musht do before you a King be. Thish deed you musht perform.'

'Thish I gotta see,' chuckled Gimlet.

Arrowroot blinked anxiously.

'Enemies? But we here are all comrades—'

'Psssst!' coached Goodgulf. 'Sorhed? Fordor? Noz-druls? The you-know-what?'

Stomper bit his lip nervously and thought.

'Well, I guess it behooves us that we march to Sorhed and challenge him, I guess.'

Goodgulf's jaw dropped with disbelief, but before he could strangle Stomper, Eorache jumped up on the table.

'Dot's telling him! Ve march against der Sorhedder und mess him up gute!'

Goodgulf's screams were lost in the roar of alcoholic approval from the hall.

It was the next morning that the armies of Twodor marched east laden with long lances, sharp swords, and death-dealing hangovers. The thousands were led by Arrowroot, who sat limply in his sidesaddle, nursing a whopper. Goodgulf, Gimlet, and the rest rode by him, praying for their fate to be quick, painless and, if possible, someone else's.

Many an hour the armies forged ahead, the war-merinos bleating under their heavy burdens and the soldiers bleating under their melting icepacks. As they drew closer to the Black Gate of Fordor, the ravages of war were seen on every side: carts overturned, villages and towns sacked and burned, billboard cuties defaced with foul black mustaches.

Arrowroot looked with darkened face at these ruins of a once fair land.

'Look at those ruins of a once fair land,' he cried, almost toppling from his sheep. 'There will be much to cleanse when we return.'

'If we ever get the chance to return,' said Gimlet, 'I'll personally clean up the whole place with a toothbrush.'

The King drew himself to a more or less upright position.

'Fear not, for our army is strong and courageous.'

'Just hope they don't sober up before we get there,' Gimlet grunted.

The dwarf's words read true, for the army began to waver in its march, and the band of Roi-Tanners Stomper charged with rounding up stragglers hadn't reported for hours.

Finally Arrowroot decided to put a stop to the malingering by shaming his hesitant warriors. Commanding the remaining herald to sound the horn he said:

'Peoples of the West! The battle before the Black Gate of Sorhed will be one of few against many; but the few are of pure heart and the many are of the filthy. Nevertheless, those of you who wish to cringe and run from the fight may do so to quicken our pace. Those who still ride with the King of Twodor will live forever in song and legend! The rest may go.'

It is said that the dustcloud did not settle for many days after.

'That was close indeed,' said Spam, still shaking from their narrow escape from Schlob a few days before. Frito nodded feebly but still could not really piece together what had happened.

Before them the great salt flats of Fordor stretched to the feet of a giant molehill which held Bardahl, the high-rise headquarters of Sorhed. The wide plain was dotted with barracks, parade grounds, and motor pools. Thousands of narcs were swarming frantically, digging holes and filling them up again and polishing the dusty ground with enormous buffers. Far in the distance the Zazu Pits, the Black Hole, spewed the sooty remains of hundreds of years of *National Geographic*s into the air over Fordor. Right before them, at the foot of the cliff, a thick, black pool of tar bubbled noisily, from time to time emitting a heavy belch.

Frito stood for a long time, peering out from under his fingers at the distant, smoking volcano.

'It's many a hard kilo to the Black Hole,' he said, fingering the Ring.

'No lie, bwana,' said Spam.

'This nearer tar pit has a certain holelike flavor,' said Frito.

'Round,' agreed Spam. 'Open. Deep.'

'Dark,' added Frito.

'Black,' said Spam.

Frito took the Ring from round his neck and twirled it absently at the end of its chain.

'Careful, Mr Frito,' said Spam, raining a series of hitsies on his arm.

'Indeed,' said Frito, flinging the Ring in the air and deftly catching it behind his back.

'Very risky,' Spam said, and picking up a large stone, he threw it into the center of the tar pit, where it sank with a wet *glop*.

'Pity we have no weight to anchor it safely to the bottom,' said Frito, swinging the chain over his head. 'Accidents can happen.'

'Just in case,' said Spam, searching vainly in his pack for some heavy object. 'A dead weight, a sinker,' he muttered.

'Hello,' said a gray lump behind them. 'Long time no see.'

'Goddam, old shoe,' crooned Spam, and dropped a coin at Goddam's feet.

'Small world,' said Frito as he palmed the Ring and clapped the surprised creature on the back.

'Look!' cried Frito, pointing to an empty sky. 'The Winged Victory of Samothrace.' And as Goddam turned to see, Frito looped the chain over his neck.

'Holla,' cried Spam, 'a 1927 Indian-head nickel!' and dropped on his hands and knees in front of Goddam.

'Whoops!' said Frito.

'Aiyeee,' added Goddam.

'Floop,' suggested the tar pit.

Frito let out a deep sigh and both boggies bade a final farewell to the Ring and its ballast. As they raced from the pit, a loud bubbling noise grew from the black depths and the earth began to tremble. Rocks split and the ground opened beneath their very feet, causing the boggies much concern. In the distance the dark towers began to crumble and Frito saw Sorhed's offices at Bardahl seam and shatter into a smoking heap of plaster and steel.

'Sure don't build 'em like they used to,' observed Spam as he dodged a falling water cooler.

Great rents appeared around the boggies and they found themselves cut off from escape. The whole land seemed to writhe and moan from its very bowels, which after eons of lethargy, had finally begun to move. The earth tipped at a crazy angle and the boggies slid toward a crevass filled with used razor blades and broken wine bottles.

'Ciao!' waved Spam to Frito.

'At a time like this?' sobbed Frito.

Then just over their heads they saw a passing flash of color. There in the sky they saw a giant eagle, full-feathered and painted shocking pink. On its side were the words DEUS EX MACHINA AIRLINES in metallic gold.

Frito yelped as the great bird swooped low and snatched them both from death with its rubberized talons.

'Name's Gwahno,' said the Eagle as they climbed sharply away from the disintegrating land. 'Find a seat.'

'But how—' began Frito.

'Not now, mac,' the bird snapped. 'Gotta figure a flight plan outta this dump.'

The powerful wings bore them to a dizzying height and Frito looked with awe upon the convulsed land below. Fordor's black rivers were twisting like ring-worms, huge glaciers figure skated across barren plains, and the mountains were playing leapfrog.

Just before Gwahno began banking a turn, Frito thought he caught a glimpse of a great, dark form the color and shape of a bread pudding retreating over the mountains with a steamer trunk of odd socks.

*

The glorious army that drew up before the Black Gate numbered somewhat less than the original thousands. It numbered seven, to be exact, and might have been less had not seven merinos finally bolted for freedom out from under their riders. Cautiously, Arrowroot looked upon the Black Gate to Fordor. It was many times a man in height and painted a flashy red. Both halves were labeled OUT.

'They will issue from here,' Arrowroot explained. 'Let us unfurl our battle standard.'

Dutifully Goodgulf fitted together his cue and attached the white cloth.

'But that is not our standard,' said Arrowroot.

'Bets?' said Gimlet.

'Better Sorhed than no head,' said Goodgulf as he bent his sword into a plowshare.

Suddenly Arrowroot's eyes bugged.

'Lo!' he cried.

Black flags were raised in the black towers and the gate opened like an angry maw to upchuck its evil spew. Out poured an army the likes of which was never seen. Forth from the gate burst a hundred thousand rabid narcs swinging bicycle chains and tire irons, followed by drooling divisions of pop-eyed change-lings, deranged zombies, and distempered werewolves. At their shoulders marched eight score heavily armored griffins, three thousand goose-stepping mummies, and a column of abominable snowmen on motorized bobsleds; at their flanks tramped six companies of slavering ghouls, eighty parched vampires in white tie, and the Phantom of the Opera. Above them the sky was blackened by the dark shapes of vicious pelicans, houseflies the size of two-car garages, and Rodan the Flying Monster. Through the portals streamed more foes of various forms and descriptions, including a six-legged diplodocus, the Loch Ness Monster, King Kong, Godzilla, the Creature from the Black Lagoon, the Beast with 1,000,000 Eyes, the Brain from Planet Arous, three different subphyla of giant insects, the Thing, It, She, Them, and the Blob. The great tumult of their charge could have waked the dead, were they not already bringing up the rear.

'Lo,' warned Stomper, 'the enemy approaches.'

Goodgulf gripped his cue with an iron hand as the others huddled around him in a last, shivering tableau before the fiendish onslaught.

'Vell, ve going bye-bye,' Eorache said as she crushed Arrowroot in a sweet, final embrace.

'Farewell,' squeaked Arrowroot. 'We will die heroes.'

'Perhaps,' sobbed Moxie, 'we shall meet in better lands than this.'

'Wouldn't be difficult,' agreed Pepsi as he made out his will.

'So long, shrimp,' Legolam said to Gimlet.

'Be seein' ya, creep,' replied the dwarf.

'*Lo!*' exclaimed Arrowroot, rising from his knees.

'If he says that once more,' said Gimlet, 'I'll croak him myself.'

But all eyes followed the Ranger-King's shaking pinkie. The sky was filling with a bright puce smog, and there came in a great wind a *blatting* noise similar to that made by certain Rings when they give up the ghost. The black ranks wavered in their march, stopped, and began to fidget. Suddenly, cries of anguish were heard from above and black pelicans fell from the sky, their Black Riders desperately struggling with ripcords. The narc hordes shrieked, threw down their tire irons, and hot-footed it toward the open gate. But as the narcs and their scaly allies turned back to safety, they were changed as if by magic into pillars of garlic. The terrible army had vanished and all that remained were a few white mice and a soggy pumpkin.

'Sorhed's army is no more!' cried Arrowroot, catching the drift.

Then a dark shadow raced along the plain. Looking up, they saw a large pink eagle circle the battleground, correct for windage, and skid to a creditable three-point landing in front of them, bearing the two haggard, yet familiar, passengers.

'Frito! Spam!' cried the seven.

'Goodgulf! Arrowroot! Moxie! Pepsi! Legolam! Gimlet! Eorache!' cried the boggies.

'Stow it,' growled Gwahno the Windlord. 'I'm already behind schedule.'

Gleefully, the rest of the company and Eorache clambered aboard the eagle's broad back, eager for the sight of Minas Troney. The great bird taxied along the plain, and, shaking some ice from his tailfeathers, bounded gracelessly into the air.

'Fastern your seatbelts,' cautioned Gwahno, looking over his wing at Arrowroot, 'and use those paper bags. That's what they're *there* for, mac.'

The reunited wayfarers soared high into the sky and caught a convenient westbound jet stream that brought them over the fair city of Minas Troney in a few short words.

'Nice tail wind today,' grunted Gwahno.

The overloaded eagle dipped its wings and crash-landed before the very gates of the seven-ringed city.

Wearily, yet happily, the company debirded and accepted the cheering adulation of the huge throngs, who tearfully pelted them with cigar bands and Rice Krispies. Arrowroot gave no thought to their praise, however; he was still using his bag. Nevertheless, a bevy of comely elf-maidens drew nigh the pre-occupied Ranger bearing a rich crown of all aluminum and set with many a sparkling aggie.

'It's the crown!' cried Frito, 'the Crown of Lafresser!'

Then the elfin honeys placed the Royal Porkpie over Stomper's eyes and robed him in the shimmering tinsel of Twodor's True King. Arrowroot opened his mouth, but the Crown slipped down around his neck and gagged his acceptance speech. The gay throngs took this as a good omen and went home. Arrowroot turned to Frito and beamed mutely. Frito bowed low at this silent thanks, but his brows were knitted with another matter.

'You have destroyed the Great Ring, and the gratitude of all Lower Middle Earth is yours,' spoke Goodgulf, clapping an approving hand on Frito's wallet. 'I now grant you one wish in payment for your heroism. All you have to do is ask.'

Frito stood on tiptoe and whispered in the kindly old Wizard's ear.

'Down the street to the left,' nodded Goodgulf. 'You can't miss it.'

So it was that the Great Ring was unmade and Sorhed's power destroyed forever. Arrowroot of Arrowshirt and Eorache soon were wedded, and the old Wizard prophesied that eight monocled and helmeted offspring would soon be smashing the palace furniture. Pleased by this, the King made Goodgulf Wizard Without

Portfolio to the newly conquered Fordorian lands and gave him a fat expense account, to be voided only if he ever decided to set foot back in Twodor. To Gimlet the dwarf, Arrowroot granted a scrap-metal franchise on Sorhed's surplus war engines; to Legolam, he granted the right to rename Chikken Noodul 'Ringland' and run the souvenir concession at the Zazu Pits. Lastly, to the four boggies he gave the Royal Handshake, and one-way tickets aboard Gwahno back to the Sty. Of Sorhed, little was heard again, though if he returned, Arrowroot promised him full amnesty and an executive position in Twodor's defense labs. Of the ballhog and Schlob, little was heard either, but local gossips reported that wedding bells were only centuries away.

X

BE IT EVER SO HORRID

It was but a short time after Stomper's coronation that Frito, still in his tattered elvin-cloak, wearily trod the familiar cattle run to Bug End. The flight had been swift, and, save some air pockets and a midair collision with a gaggle of migrating flamingos, quite uneventful.

Boggietown was a filthy mess. Piles of unclaimed garbage littered the soupy streets and bloated boggie-brats somehow managed to track their goo up the tree trunks; no one had even bothered to clean up the litter from Dildo's party. Frito found himself oddly pleased that so little had changed during his absence.

'Been away?' croaked a familiar voice.

'Yes,' said Frito, spitting at old Fatlip with traditional boggie formality. 'I am home from the Great War. I have unmade the Ring of Power and vanquished Sorhed, evil ruler of far Fordor.'

'Do tell,' sniggered Fatlip as he made a thorough search of a nostril. 'Wondered where you got the queer duds.'

Frito passed on to his own hole and waded through a mound of papers and milk bottles to his door. Inside, he made a fruitless inspection of his icebox and returned to his den to make a small fire. Then he tossed his elvin-cloak into a corner and collapsed with a sigh into his easy chair. He had seen much, and now he was home.

Just then a soft knocking came at the door.

'Dammit,' muttered Frito, roused from his reveries. 'Who's there?'

There was no reply save another, more insistent knock.

'Okay, okay, I'm coming,' Frito went to the door and opened it.

There on the stoop were twenty-three lyre-strumming nymphs in gauzy pants-suits couched in a golden canoe borne on the cool mists of a hundred fire extinguishers and crewed by a dozen tipsy leprechauns uniformed in shimmering middy-blouses and fringed toreador pants. Facing Frito was a twelve-foot specter shrouded in red sateen, shod in bejeweled riding boots, and mounted on an obese, pale-blue unicorn. Around him fluttered winged frogs, miniature Valkyries, and an airborne caduceus. The tall figure offered Frito a six-fingered hand which held a curiously inscribed identification bracelet simply crawling with mysterious portents.

'I understand,' said the stranger solemnly, 'that you undertake quests.'

Frito banged the door shut in the specter's surprised

face, bolted, barred, and locked it, swallowing the key for good measure. Then he walked directly to his cozy fire and slumped in the chair. He began to muse upon the years of delicious boredom that lay ahead. Perhaps he would take up Scrabble.